Understanding English Phonetics

Theory and Practice for Koreans

전 은 Jun Eun

Shinasa

Understanding English Phonetics:
Theory and Practice for Koreans

First Published August 2009
Second Published July 2012
SHINASA Publishing Co.
28-36 NokBeon-Dong, EunPyung-Gu, Seoul, Korea
Registered : 9-52 (Jan. 5 1956)
Tel : 02-382-6411
Fax : 02-382-6401
E-mail : shinasa@chol.com / Homepage : www.shinasa.co.kr

ISBN : 978-89-8396-654-4

Printed and bounded in Korea

₩ **10,000**

Contents

Sounds can be downloaded at library section of author's homepage: http://knuenglish.co.kr/gnu4/pro_6.htm

Also available at publisher's homepage: http://shinasa.co.kr

1. Organs of Speech

Speech is pivotal in human communication. Speech functions as primary communication, making up of most of our communication. The components that consist of speech are sounds, which are called speech sounds. The speech sounds are essential elements when we speak and listen.

Phonetics is the study of speech sounds produced in languages. It researches what these sounds are, how they are produced, what their acoustic properties are, and how they are adjusted according to their surrounding environments. Its main task is to find out what aspects of the sounds work to convey the meaning of what is being said. English Phonetics is concerned with speech sounds used in the English language. This book focuses on English Phonetics. The analysis and description will be made with regard to the properties of English speech sounds.

If Koreans are to understand English speech sounds well, it is helpful to compare them with the speech sounds of the Korean language. This book describes English speech sounds with the aim of helping Koreans understand and acquire them. English speech sounds will be considered in comparison with Korean speech sounds.

1.1 The Production of Speech

First we need to consider how English speech sounds are made.

All English speech sounds are produced on an outgoing breath. They talk while breathing out. English speech is superimposed on an outgoing breath. The basic source for sounds is air while being exhaled.[1)]

Let us look at the journey of air when we are exhaling. First air starts from the lungs and goes up the trachea. At the top of the trachea we have a larynx. Within the larynx there is an important structure named vocal folds. The opening of the vocal folds is called the glottis. The air passes through the larynx and the glottis. Then it goes up the pharynx and passes through the oral cavity or the nasal cavity, going outside. Look at the following figure 1.1.

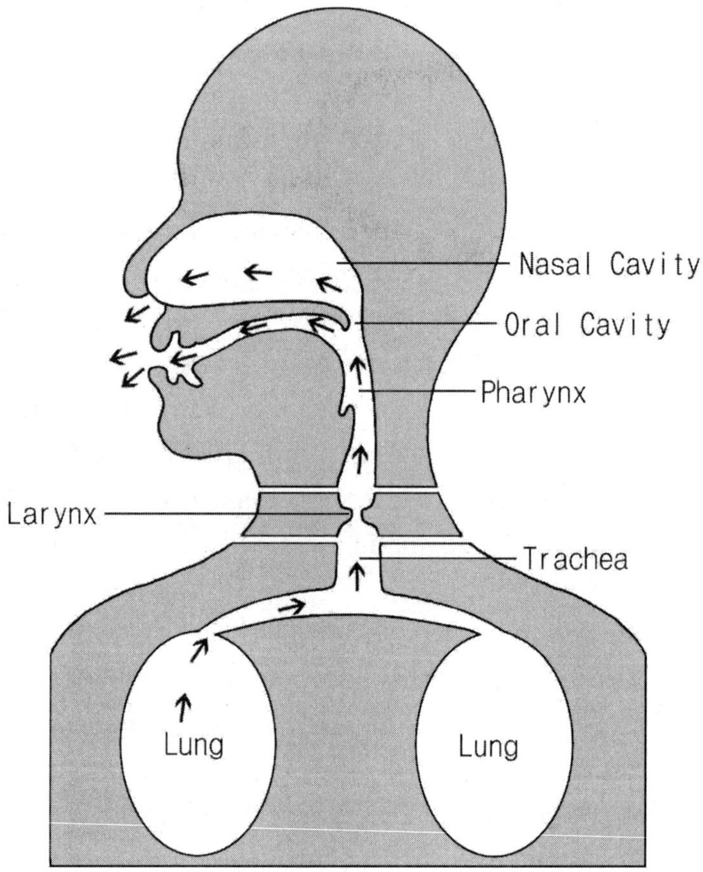

Figure 1.1 The journey of air from the lung

---

1) Sounds produced in this way are said to be made by a pulmonic egressive airstream mechanism.

When we are breathing out, the vocal folds are apart, which is the default state. The air has relatively free passage into the pharynx and the mouth. However, when we talk, we nearly close the vocal folds and make them vibrate. This is the main source of sound waves.

1.2 The Vocal Organs

In phonetics, the air passage above the larynx is named the vocal tract. The shape of the vocal tract is a very important factor because the shape changes to make different sounds. The parts of the vocal tract work to form different shapes. These different parts are called articulators. Two articulators are usually involved when forming sounds: the upper part and the lower one. Try saying the word '*play*'. The upper lip and the lower lip come together in the formation of *p* and then come apart. The tongue tip is raised and pressed to the upper mouth roof for the *l* and then comes down for the following vowel.

The names of the upper parts are given in Figure 1.2. The upper lip and the upper teeth are familiar. A small ridge just behind the upper teeth is called the alveolar ridge, which you can feel with the tip of the tongue. Behind this the roof of the mouth is curved and hard. This is the hard palate. Behind the hard palate there is the soft palate or velum at the back of the mouth. Most people cannot curl the tongue enough to touch it. The soft palate is literally soft and movable. Usually there is an opening between the soft palate and the pharynx wall, so the air can pass through the nose. However, if the soft palate is raised and pressed against the back wall of the pharynx, air cannot escape through the nose but only through the mouth. This is how oral sounds are produced. At the lower end of the soft palate there is an appendage hanging down, which is known as the uvula. The pharynx is the tube between the uvula and the larynx.

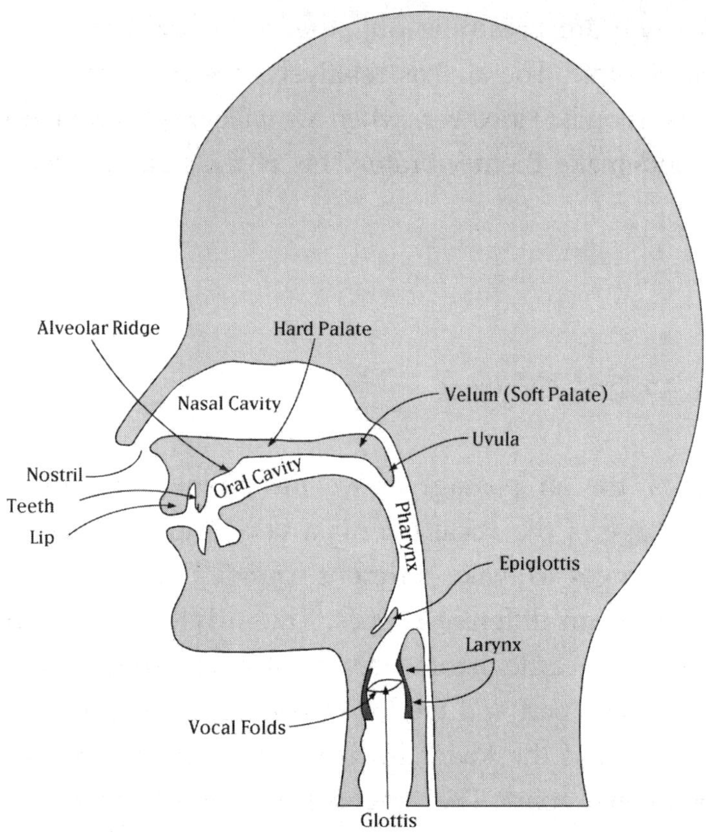

Figure 1.2 The upper part of the vocal tract

The lower lip and the tongue form the lower articulators of the vocal tract. The tongue is a very important articulator and it moves into many different places, forming different shapes. The tongue is divided into different parts with specific names: tip, blade, front, back, and root. The fore-part of the tongue is the blade, not the front tongue. The front tongue is located behind the blade despite what its name implies. The name may mislead us about its place. The front tongue and the back tongue make up the body of the tongue. The front tongue is a front part of the body of the tongue. Roughly the blade of the tongue lies underneath the alveolar ridge, the front tongue underneath the hard palate, and the back tongue underneath the soft palate when the tongue is at rest. The remainder of the tongue is the root. The tip and blade of the tongue are the most mobile parts. The epiglottis is attached to the lower part of the root of the tongue. It protects the larynx and prevents food from going into the larynx when we swallow. Refer to Figure 1.3.

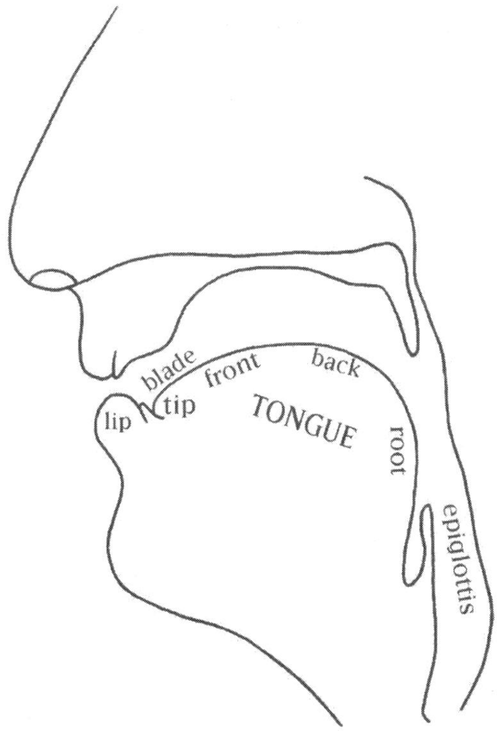

Figure 1.3 The lower parts of the vocal tract

So far we have considered the parts of the vocal organs involved in the production of speech and their names. Some terminology is familiar, but some is new. We should become familiar with these terms in order to understand how speech sounds are articulated.

1.3 Exercise

1. Write the names of the vocal organs in the spaces provided.

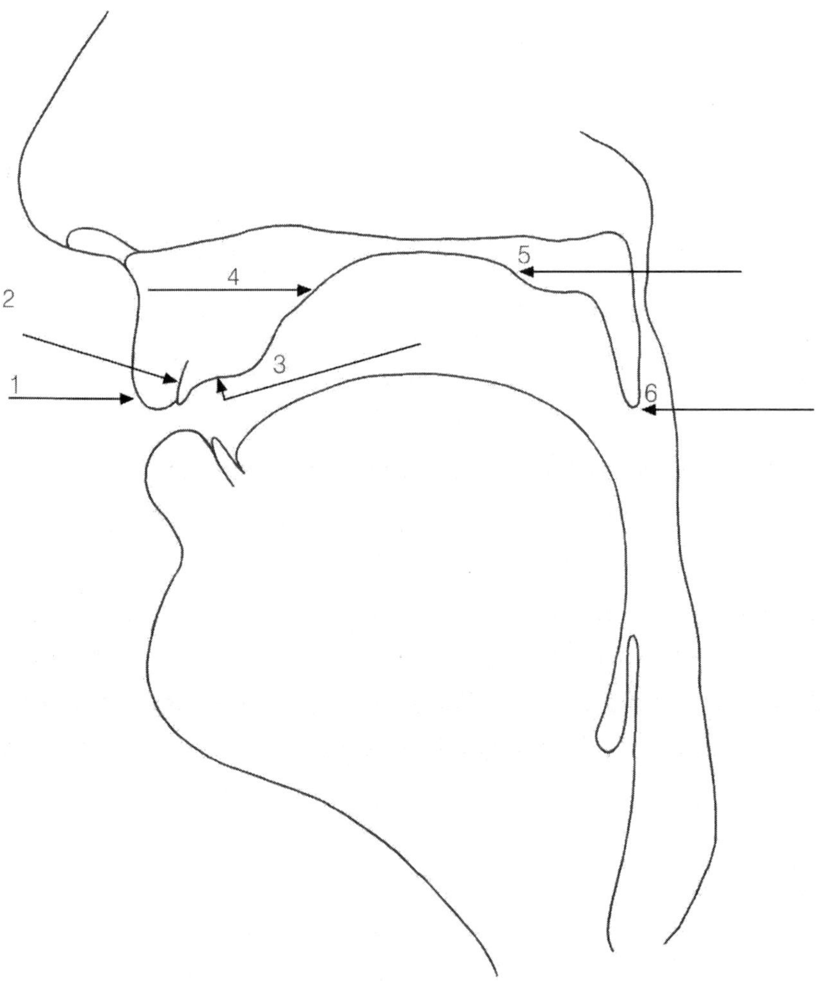

Figure 1.4

2. Write the names of the vocal organs in the spaces provided.

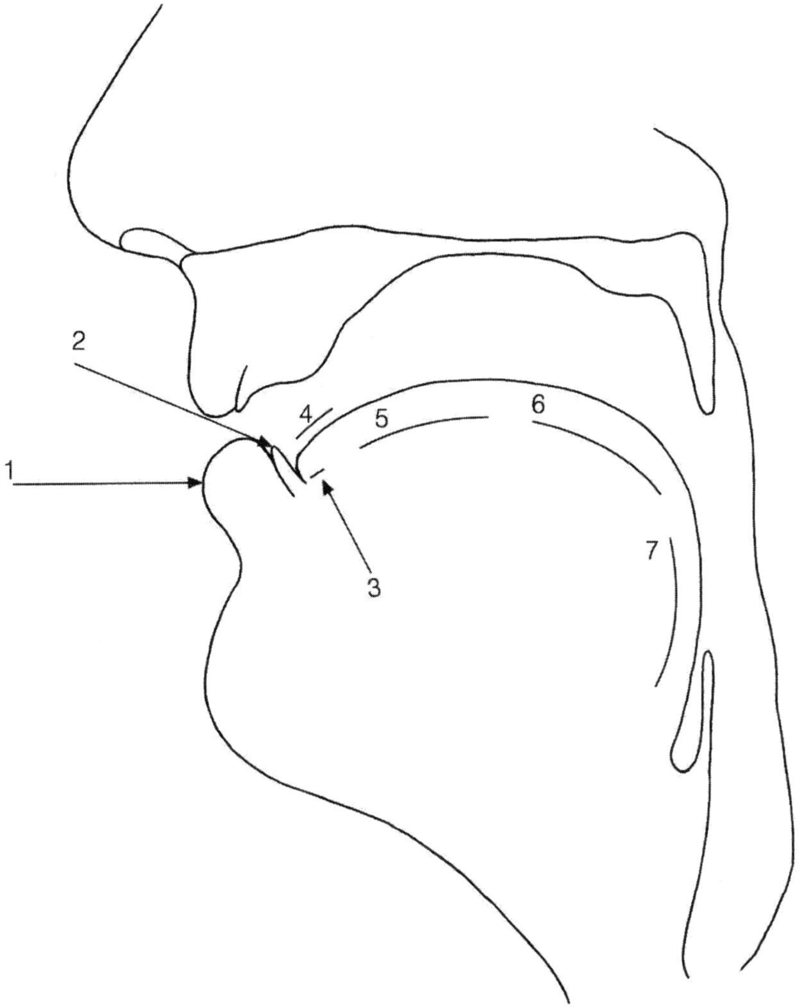

Figure 1.4

2. Description of English Consonants

Before we look at English consonants, let us consider what factor distinguishes consonants and vowels. What is it that makes some speech sounds vowels and other speech sounds consonants? Consonants are speech sounds that are produced with a blocking of the passage of air in the vocal tract by articulators, while vowels are sounds produced with a relatively open vocal tract.

The obstruction of the airstream is necessary to form consonants. Therefore, consonants are classified according to where the airstream is constricted (the place of articulation) and how the airstream is constricted (the manner of articulation). Another aspect for English consonants is whether the consonant is voiced or voiceless. Sounds which are constricted both at the same place and by the same way may result in different sounds according to the voicedness like *p* and *b* (*pill* and *bill*). In the description of English consonants, three different aspects of the articulation are to be considered:

1. Where is the airstream constricted?
2. How is the airstream constricted?
3. Is the sound voiced or voiceless?

2.1 Places of Articulation

As for places of articulation, where the vocal tract is made more narrow, the followings are used in the description of English consonants.

① **Bilabial**

Bilabial sounds are made by bringing both lips closer together. There are four such sounds in English: [p](*pie*), [b](*buy*), [m](*my*), [w](*way*). Note how the lips come together for the first sound in each of these words.

② **Labiodental**

Labiodental consonants are made with the lower lip nearly touching the upper front teeth. English has two labiodental sounds: [f](*fine*) and [v](*vine*).

③ **Interdental**

Interdental sounds are made with the tip of the tongue between the front teeth. The tip of the tongue usually is placed below the upper front teeth. There are two interdental sounds in English: [θ](*think*) and [ð](*then*).

④ **Alveolar**

Alveolar sounds are made with tongue tip or blade at or near the alveolar ridge. The alveolar ridge is easiest to make an approach, not too forward neither too backward. Also the tip or blade of the tongue is the most mobile part of the tongue. Therefore the number of consonants which are articulated in this place is the largest. In English, there are seven such consonants: [t](*tie*), [d](*day*), [s](*see*), [z](*zoo*), [l](*lie*), [r](*right*), and [n](*night*).
The sound made with the tip of the tongue raised toward the alveolar ridge is said to be retroflex. The initial sound [r] of the word '*red*' is retroflex. Speakers of American English use retroflex sounds.

⑤ Palato-Alveolar

The roof of our mouth is curved behind the alveolar ridge and the anterior portion is hard. Sounds made with tongue blade near the hard part of the roof of the mouth are called palato-alveolar. There are four palato-alveolar sounds in English: [ʃ](*ship*), [ʒ] (measure), [ʧ](*church*), and [ʤ](*juice*).

⑥ Palatal

The sound made with the front raised toward the hard palate is said to be palatal. The initial sound [y] of the word '*yes*' is palatal. Sometimes palatal-alveolar sounds and palatal sounds are not distinguished and are all called palatal.

⑦ Velar

The soft part of the roof of the mouth behind the hard palate is called the velum. Sounds made with the back tongue raised toward the velum are called velar. There are three velar sounds in English: [k](*king*), [g](*girl*), [ŋ] (*sing*).

⑧ Glottal

The opening between the vocal folds is the glottis. Sounds made at the glottis is said to be glottal. English has one glottal sound: [h](*hello*).

2.2 Exercise

The arrows in the following figure indicate the places of the articulation for consonants. Write the places of articulation in the spaces provided below.

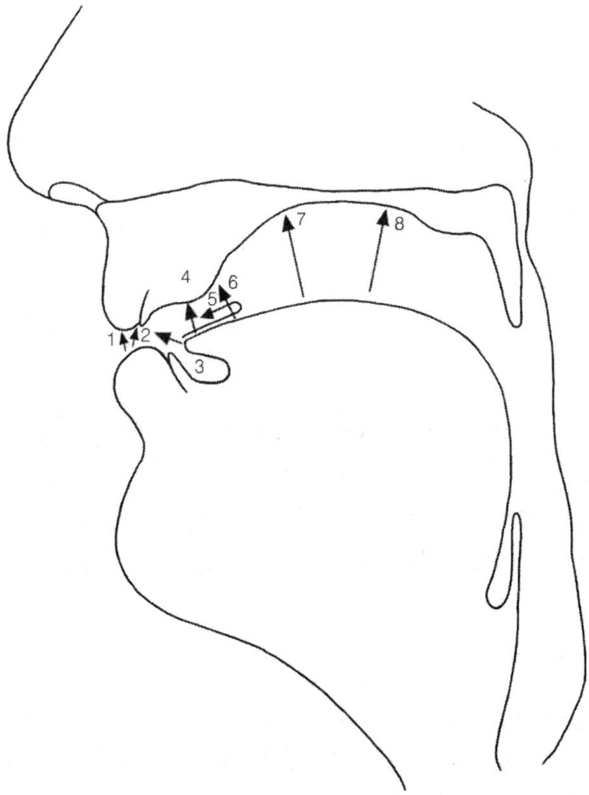

1.	______________________	5.	______________________
2.	______________________	6.	______________________
3.	______________________	7.	______________________
4.	______________________	8.	______________________

2.3 Manners of Articulation

Besides stating where the airstream is constricted, it is also necessary to describe the manner of the articulation, how it is constricted to produce consonants. The manner of the articulation of a sound is dependent on the degree of closure of the articulators. The articulators may completely close the vocal tract or they may approximate, or just narrow the tract a little.

① Stops

Stops are made by stopping the airstream completely in the oral cavity. When the articulators are held completely closed, air pressure will build up. As the articulators separate rapidly, the compressed air will burst out. There are 3 stages of articulation for stops as in Figure 2.2 : the closing stage where the articulator is closing the tract, the holding stage where the articulators remain in contact and the air pressure increases, and the releasing stage where the compressed air is released at the same time the articulators come apart.

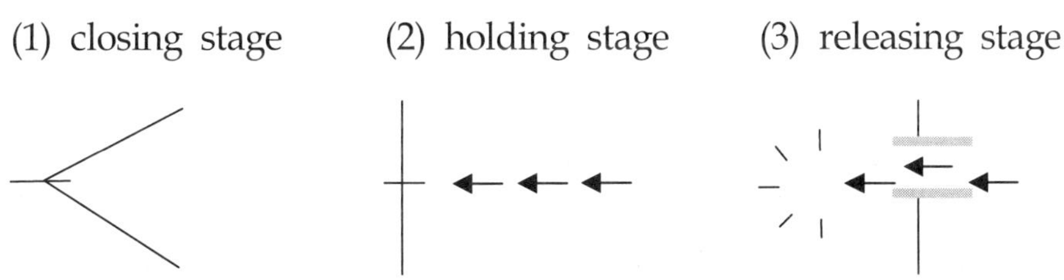

Figure 2.2

When stops are released, they are usually accompanied by air burst called plosion. Thus they are also called *plosives* named after such audible characteristics. English has three pairs of stops: [p]/[b], [t]/[d], [k]/[g]. They are all the same in that a complete closure is made in the mouth, but they sound different according to where the closure is made. [p]/[b] are bilabial, [t]/[d] alveolar, and [k]/ [g] velar. When you say [p] or [b], your lips are closed together for a moment, stopping the airflow. [p] is a voiceless bilabial and [b] is a voiced bilabial.

② **Fricatives**

Fricative sounds are made by nearly stopping the airstream. The opening is very small and the air is forced out through a narrow passage between the articulators, resulting in considerable friction. The air flows continuously and the release is continuant. English has 9 fricative sounds: [f], [v], [θ], [ð], [s], [z], [ʃ], [ʒ], [h]. Korean has only 3 fricative sounds: [ㅅ], [ㅆ], [ㅎ]. When learning English, Koreans face many new fricative sounds, which is a challenge for them.

(1) approximating stage (2) releasing stage

Figure 2.3

[f] and [v] are labiodental. They are produced by almost stopping the air with the lower lip in contact with the upper teeth. [θ] and [ð] are dental (or interdental). They are made by nearly blocking the air with the tongue tip beneath the upper teeth. The air is blown out through the gap between the tongue and the teeth.

[s] and [z] are alveolar fricatives which are made at the same place as [t] and [d]. They differ in their manner of articulation. While a complete blockage of the air is made in [t] and [d] by pressing the tongue tip against the alveolar ridge, a near blockage of the air is made in [s] and [z] by almost closing the tongue tip against the alveolar ridge with-

out touching it. The air is forced out through the narrow opening.

[ʃ] and [ʒ] are palato-alveolar. They are produced by raising the blade of the tongue to be close to the back part of the alveolar ridge.

As for [h], its place of articulation is glottal. [h] is produced by narrowing the vocal folds. When the air is forced out through them, the friction noise is made.

③ Affricates

In English there are two affricates: [ʧ] and [ʤ]. As implied in their phonetic symbols, their production involves two manners of articulation. They can be thought of as a combination of a stop and a fricative. At the beginning the air is completely stopped briefly like a stop and then the air is released like a fricative. In stops, articulators obstruct the air and then open wide. In affricates, after the air is stopped, the articulators open only enough to make a narrow opening. The air is released through the narrow opening, making friction.

(1) closing stage

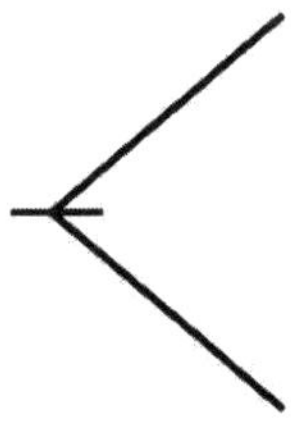

(2) releasing stage

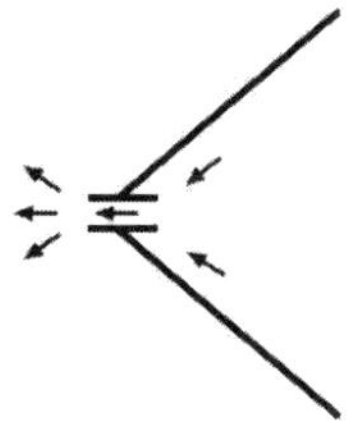

Figure 2.4

In [ʧ] and [ʤ], their place of articulation is palato-alveolar. To make them, the blade of the tongue is raised to make contact with the back part of the alveolar ridge, forming a stop closure. Then this contact is slackened and the air is released as in [ʃ] or [ʒ].

④ Nasals

Our soft palate can be raised or lowered. During normal breathing it is usually lowered. In nasal consonants, the air escapes through the nose and the soft palate is lowered. In the case of all the other consonants and all vowels, the soft palate is raised against the wall of the pharynx and air cannot pass through the nose. Sounds made with the soft palate raised are called oral sounds. We cannot move our nose or change the shape of our nasal cavity. Different kinds of nasal sounds are made according to the place where the air is stopped in the oral cavity. Thus they are sometimes called nasal stops.

There are three types of complete obstruction in the oral cavity for nasals: bilabial, alveolar and velar. Three nasal consonants are produced in this set of places: [m], [n], [ŋ].

[m] is made with the soft palate lowered and a complete obstruction at the lips. For [n], the velum is lowered with the tongue blade pressed against the alveolar ridge. [ŋ] is produced with the velum lowered and the back tongue stopping the airstream in the velar region. The difference between [m] and [b] is that the velum is lowered for the articulation of [m], but raised for the articulation of [b].

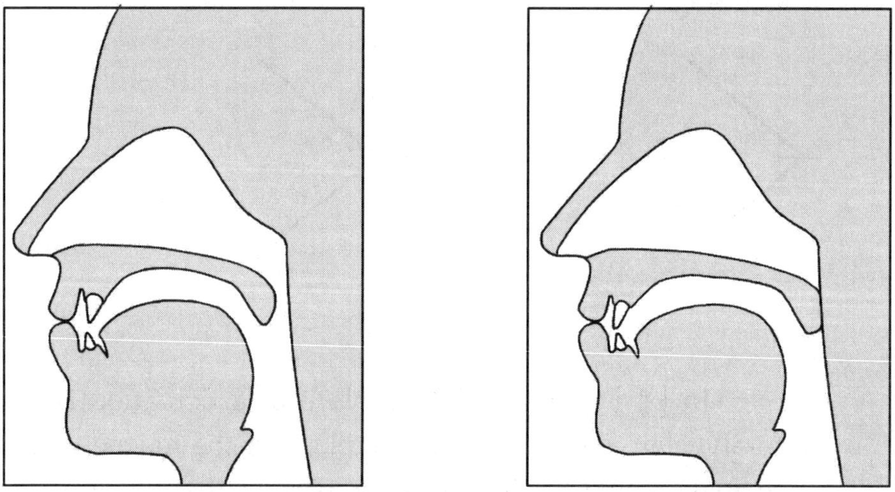

/m/ /b/

Figure 2.5

⑤ Liquids

There are two liquids in English: [l] and [r]. When a liquid is produced, there is an obstruction, but it is not so narrow as in stops, fricatives, and affricates. The passage of the airstream is comparatively wider than those and the air flows out smoothly without making plosion or friction.

[l] is called a lateral liquid. For [l], the passage of air does not go along the center of the tongue as in the usual way. Instead, there is complete closure of the center by the tongue blade pressed against the alveolar ridge. The air is laterally emitted over the sides of the tongue.

For [r], there are considerable differences in the ways speakers of English make r-sounds, but most are articulated in the alveolar region. In a common type of American English [r], the blade is raised with the tip curled backward. The tip is pointing to the area behind the alveolar ridge. This is why it is also called retroflex. It is important in the articulation of [r] not to make contact with any part of the roof of the mouth when the tip of the tongue approaches the alveolar area. The curling-back process usually carries the tip of the tongue to a position which is slightly further back than that for alveolar consonants. This is why it is sometimes called "post-alveolar".

⑥ Glides

Glides are made with only a slight closure of the articulators, so they have also been called semi-vowels or semi-consonants. In English there are two glides: [y](*yes*) and [w](*wet*). Each of these glide sounds is closely associated with a specific vowel: [y] with [i] and [w] with [u].

[y] is made with a slight closure in the palatal region. It begins at or near the [i] position, but quickly glides into the following articulation position. It is classified as a palatal glide.

[w] is made by raising the back tongue toward the velum while rounding the lip at the same time. It is classified as a bilabial/velar glide.

2.4 Vibration of the Vocal Folds

English consonants are distinguished according to the vibration of the vocal folds. The larynx is at the top of the trachea. The structure of the larynx is made of two large cartilages, which are hollow. You can feel the front of the larynx which is commonly called the Adam's Apple, in the front of your neck. The vocal folds are inside the larynx. The vocal folds are made of two thick flaps of muscle. Both of the vocal folds are joined together at the front of the neck and fixed to the inside of the thyroid cartilage. But at the back they are separated and attached to arytenoid cartilages whose movement causes the closing and opening of the vocal folds. The term glottis is used to refer to the opening between the vocal folds. A flap of tissue called epiglottis is at the front of the larynx, protecting the vocal folds.

If the vocal folds are left apart and the glottis is open, the air passes through it freely, which happens during our normal breathing and during voiceless consonants. At other times, the vocal folds are nearly closed, blocking the air stream and causing the pressure of air below it to build up. If the air pressure gets bigger than the muscle force exerted in the closing of the vocal folds, the vocal folds will yield and open. When the vocal folds are open, the clogged air will pass out. After the clogged air is gone, little air is left there and the air pressure falls. Then the muscle force becomes bigger than the air pressure force, enabling the vocal folds to be approximated. This process of the closing and opening of the vocal folds repeats very rapidly, for example, hundred times a second, making the vocal folds vibrate and producing sound waves.

Sounds made with the vocal folds vibrating are called voiced sounds. Sounds made without such vibration are called voiceless sounds. In English, all the vowels are voiced. Among the consonants, nasals (/m, n, ŋ/), liquids (/l, r/), and glides (/y, w/) are voiced.

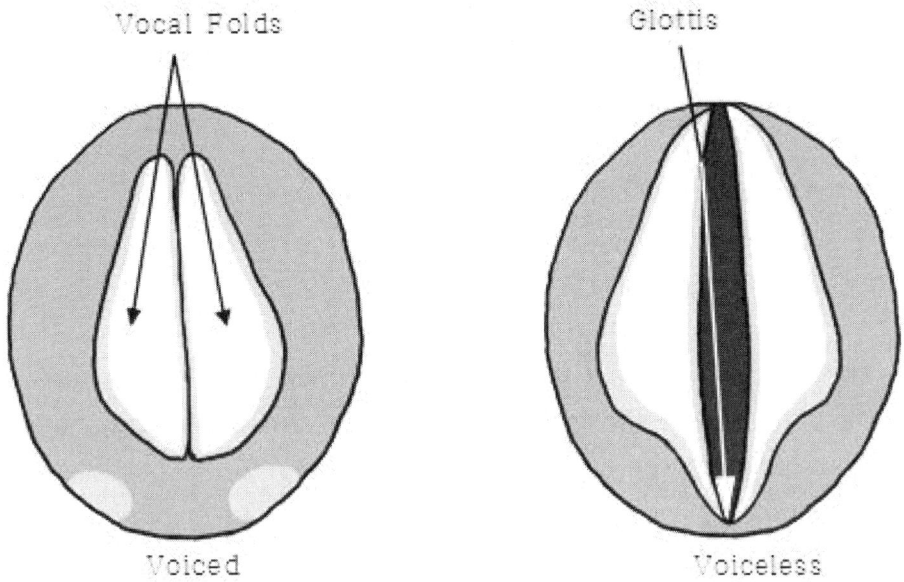

Figure 2.6

However, stops, fricatives (except /h/), and affricates show oppositions with regard to voicing, coming in voiced and voiceless ones. For example, /p/ and /b/ are bilabial stops, made both at the same place and in the same way. They differ only in the voicing. /p/ is a voiceless bilabial stop, while /b/ is a voiced bilabial stop. The presence or absence of the voicing determines a different sound. English consonants are patterned in opposition for the voiceless sounds and the counterpart voiced ones as follows:

voiceless		voiced	
/p/	pill	/b/	bill
/t/	tip	/d/	dip
/k/	cold	/g/	gold
/f/	fine	/v/	vine
/θ/	smooth	/ð/	smoothe
/s/	seal	/z/	zeal
/ʃ/	leash	/ʒ/	esion
/ʧ/	chew	/ʤ/	jew

Voiceless consonants are normally more strongly articulated, held, and articulated with greater energy and pressure than their voiced counterparts. Voiceless consonants tend to be fortis sounds, while voiced consonants tend to be lenis or weak sounds.

2.5 Chart of English Consonants

So far we have looked at English consonants in terms of three aspects of the articulation: the place, the manner, and the voicing, which is represented in the following chart.

Manner of Articulation	Place of Articulation													
	Bilabial		Labiodental		Interdental		Alveolar		Palatal		Velar		Glottal	
	vl	vd	vl	vd	vl	vd	vl	vd	vl	vd	vl	vd	vl	vd
Stop	p	b					t	d			k	g		
Fricative			f	v	θ	ð	s	z	ʃ	ʒ			h	
Affricate									ʧ	ʤ				
Nasal		m						n				ŋ		
Lateral								l						
Retroflex								r						
Glide		w								y		(w)		

(*vl = voiceless, vd = voiced)

Figure 2.7 The Consonants of English

The label at the top of the vertical column shows the place of articulation and the label at the left of the horizontal row indicates the manner of articulation. Locate [z], for example. It lies under *vd* column indicating that it is voiced. Now look above. It is in the vertical column marked alveolar. Looking to the far left, you see it is a fricative. [z], then, is a *voiced alveolar fricative*. By reverse procedure we can find a sound with a particular description. If we want to find the *voiced velar stop*, first look under the *velar* column, then in the *stop* row, and locate the symbol under the *vd* column: this is [g]. With the chart, we can also find classes of sounds easily, such as all the velars or all the stops. All the stops are all the sounds in the *stop* row: [p], [b], [t], [d], [k], and [g]. If we are to understand English consonants, we should familiarize ourselves with this chart.

2.6 Exercise

1. Write the phonetic symbol for the sound that could be produced by the shape of the vocal tract.

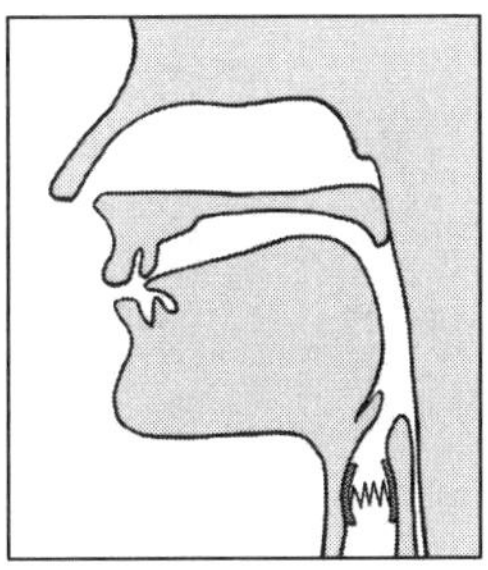

(   )

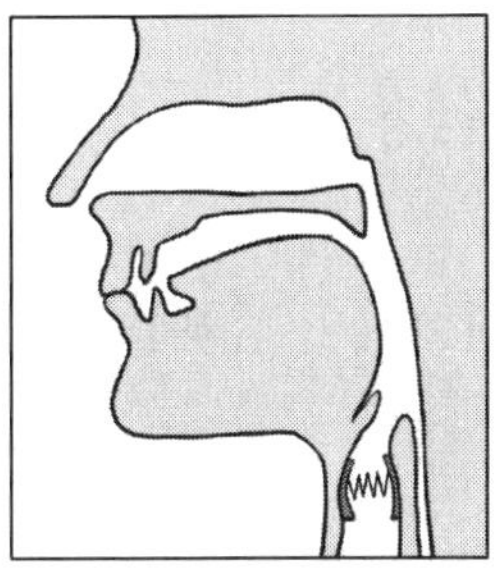

(   )

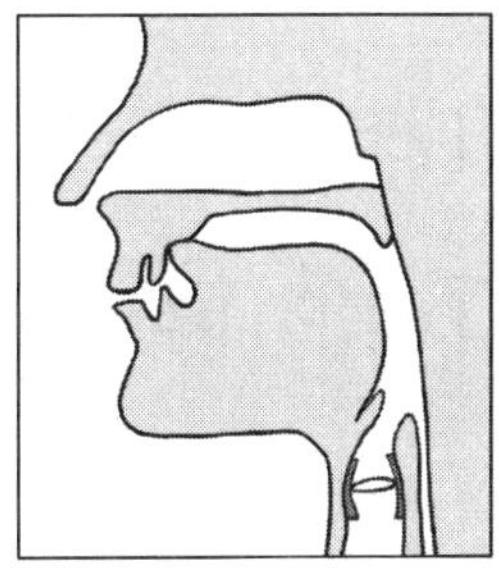

(   )

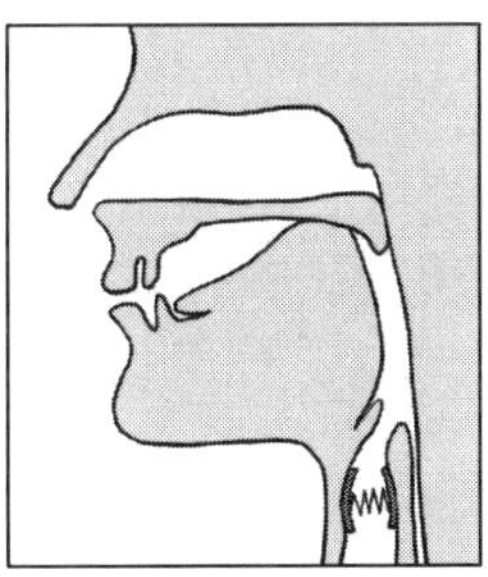

(   )

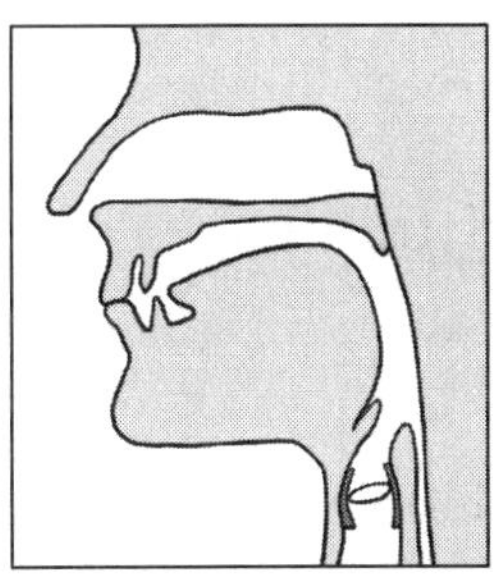

(   )

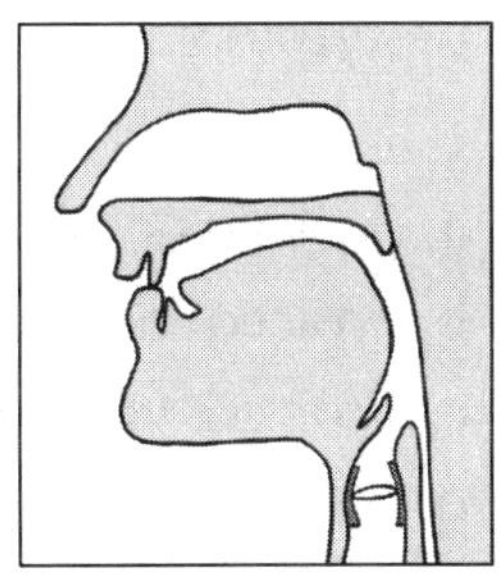

(   )

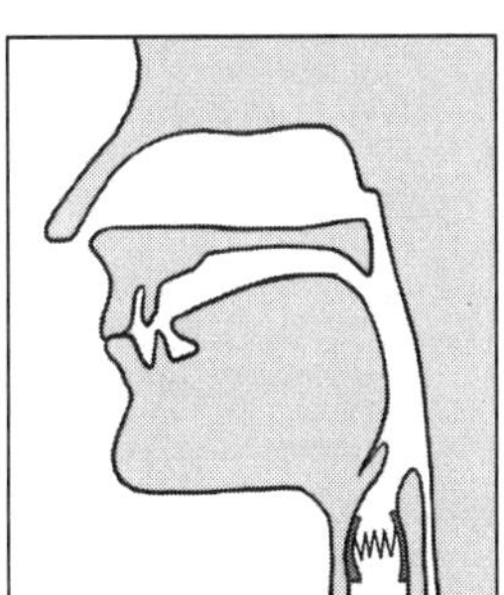

(   )

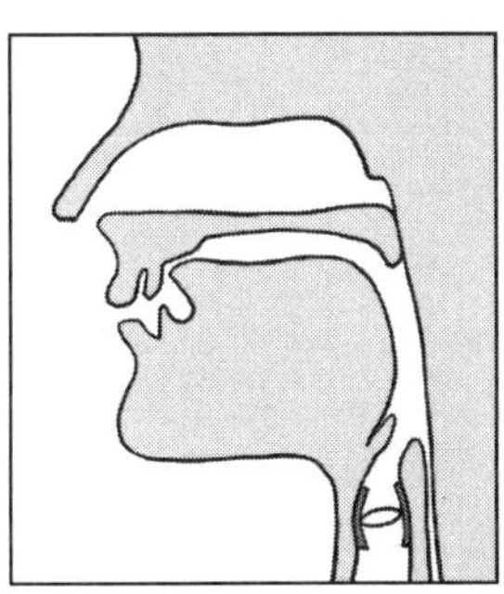

(   )

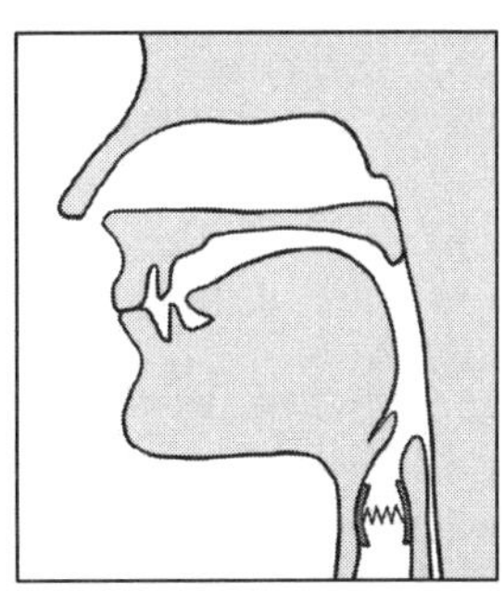

(   )

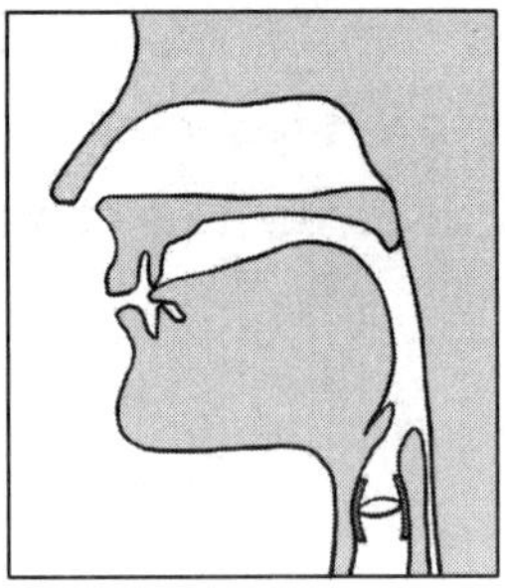 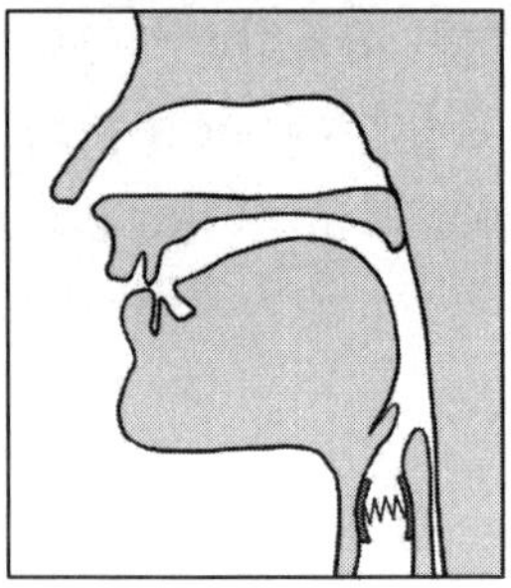 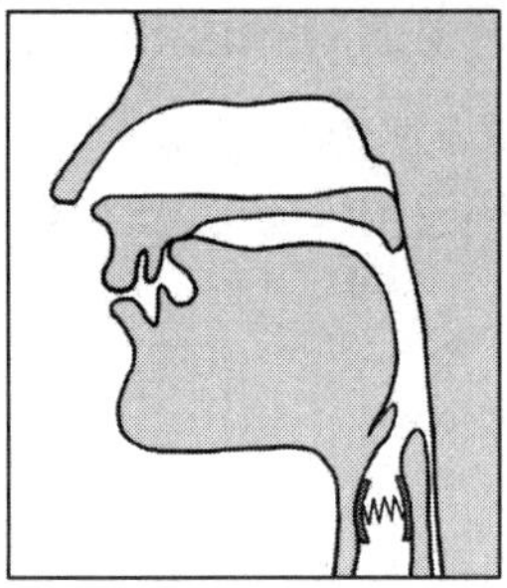

(   )   (   )   (   )

2. Circle all the symbols below which represent voiced sounds.

[z]   [f]   [h]   [y]   [l]   [s]   [g]

[d]   [b]   [p]   [m]   [θ]   [ʧ]   [ʃ]

3. Provide the phonetic symbol which is represented by the following descriptors.

a. voiceless labiodental fricative
b. voiced palatal affricate
c. voiced velar nasal
d. voiceless interdental fricative
e. voiceless palatal fricative
f. voiced alveolar retroflex

4. Provide the appropriate three-part articulatory descriptions for the consonant sounds.

a. [t]
b. [w]
c. [l]
d. [s]
e. [p]
f. [n]
g. [ʒ]
h. [ʧ]

5. Fill in the chart of English Consonants.

	vl	vd	vl	vd	vl	vd	vl	vd	vl	vd	vl	vd	vl	vd

(*vl = voiceless, vd = voiced)

The Consonants of English

3. Phonemes and Allophones

We have considered English consonants so far. Phonetically speaking, consonants are among phonemes. A phoneme is a minimal phonetic unit that triggers difference in meaning in opposition with other sounds. For example, the difference in meaning between *pig* and *big* is due to the difference in sounds between *p* and *b*. When considered as phonemes in English, *p* and *b* are written inside / / : /p/ and /b/. The two words *pig* and *big* differ only in one sound. Such pairs are called minimal pairs. They clearly show what sounds qualify as phonemes. For Koreans, '달', '딸', and '탈' are different in meaning and the difference is caused by the sound /ㄷ/, /ㄸ/, and /ㅌ/. /ㄷ/, /ㄸ/, and /ㅌ/ are phonemes in Korean.

A phoneme is psychologically real. It means that a phoneme is not a physical unit. It is a psychological entity that is recognized in our cognition system. Though /ㄷ/, /ㄸ/, and /ㅌ/ constitute three separate phonemes in Korean, English native speakers perceive these three kinds of sounds as one phoneme, /t/.

The phoneme /ㄷ/ occurs in both Korean words, '다리' and '바다'. It occurs initially in '다리' and at intervocalic position in '바다'. The /ㄷ/ in '다리' and '바다' are recognized as the same consonant. But phonetically /ㄷ/ in '바다' is voiced, while /ㄷ/ in '다리' is not. Such sounds are allophones of a phoneme. Allophones are variations of a phoneme, which are phonetically realized according to their environments. They are represented by using [ ]. /ㄷ/ has two allophones: [voiced ㄷ] and [ㄷ]. Phonetically, [voiced

ㄷ] and [ㄷ] are different, but Koreans recognize them as one and the same phoneme, /ㄷ/. Koreans usually do not discern their phonetic differences.

Allophones of one phoneme are associated with their own specific environments. That is, allophones are realized in their own specific environments such as initial, final or, intervocalic position. For example, [voiced ㄷ] occurs at intervocalic position and [ㄷ] at other positions. The environments of allophones of one phoneme do not overlap. This kind of distribution is called *complementary distribution.*

If we do not pronounce a right allophone in a given environment and pronounce another allophone instead, it does not cause a difference in meaning. For example, if we say a voiced [ㄷ] in '다리', although it does not seem to happen in a normal situation for Koreans, it does not lead to a difference in meaning, but conveys the same meaning. This aspect shows how allophones and phonemes differ. Allophones of one phoneme are in free variation relation with each other because substitution of one allophone for another allophone does not cause a difference in meaning, unlike the case with phonemes.

Allophones of one phoneme share phonetic similarity. Even though [h] occurs initially and [ŋ] finally, so they occur in complementary distribution, but they do not form allophones, because they are phonetically too different to belong to one and the same phoneme.

3.1 Aspirated Stops

In English, [p] of *pat* and [p] of *spat* are both recognized as the same phoneme, /p/. But the two [p]s are phonetically different as in [voiced ㄷ] and [ㄷ] in Korean. [p] of *pat* is pronounced with a puff of air accompanying it, but not for [p] of *spat*. This puff of air is called aspiration. It is transcribed with a superscripted [^{h}] like this: [p^hæt]. Aspiration occurs in all voiceless oral stops acting as the first sound in a stressed syllable in English. This is formulated as follows:

$$/p, t, k/ \rightarrow [p^h, t^h, k^h] \;/\; [_{\sigma_s} \_\_\_\_$$

(i) → means 'occur as, become, change into'
(ii) / means 'in the environment'
(iii) [means 'boundary'
(iv) σ means 'syllable'
(v) σ_s means 'stressed syllable'

[p, t, k] in *spy, stop, sky* are called unaspirated stops, when preceded by /s/ in the same syllable.

Aspirated stops		Unaspirated stops	
[p^h]	peak	[p]	spy
[t^h]	top	[t]	stop
[k^h]	cup	[k]	sky

In the case of voiceless stops, the vibration of the vocal folds of the following vowel is delayed. Duration from the moment of the release of the stop until the moment when the vibration of the vocal folds of the following vowel begins is called *voice onset time*. As for aspirated stops, voice onset time is substantial, as shown in the following figure.

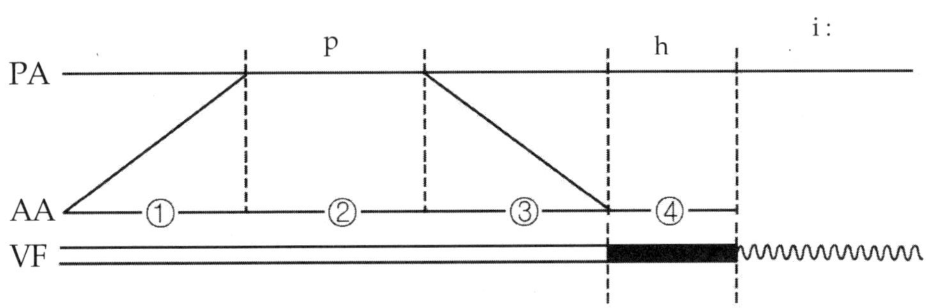

Figure 4.1 VOT in /p/, as in *pea*

VF = vocal folds
PA = passive articulator
AA = active articulator
① = closing stage
② = holding stage
③ = releasing stage
④ = VOT

3.2 Unreleased Stops

Stops may be unreleased at the end of a word as in *cap, cat, cook.* Releasing of stops are optional at word final, though unreleased stops are common. However, a stop is obligatorily unreleased when it occurs before another stop as in *action, factor, pumpkin.* We transcribe it using a superscripted [˺]

action	[æk˺ʃən]
factor	[fæk˺tɚ]
pumpkin	[pʌmp˺kɪn]

3.3 Velarized [ɫ]

The words *leaf* and *feel* both have [l] sounds. However, the [l] sounds in these two words are not identical in English. The [l] in *feel* is velarized, while the [l] of *leaf* is clear. Velarized [l]s are also called dark [l]. Velarized [l] is transcribed as [ɫ] and clear [l] as [l]. For velarized [l]s, velarizing is added to the articulation of [l]. That is, the back tongue is raised toward the velum as well as the tongue blade being pressed against the alveolar ridge so that the air is laterally emitted over the sides of the tongue. Velarized [l]s occur when they follow vowels, either at the end of a word or before a word-final consonant, that is, at syllable-final. Elsewhere clear [l]s are produced such as at syllable- initial positions and before vowels.

Velarized [ɫ]

feel	[fiyɫ]
pill	[pɪɫ]
kill	[kɪɫ]

Clear [l]

line	[layn]
life	[layf]
light	[layt]

3.4 Flaps

In American English, /t/ and /d/ are pronounced as a flap in intervocalic position (between vowels). The flap is produced when the tongue tip hits the alveolar ridge at a high speed. It is transcribed as [ɾ]. The flap also occurs in Korean and [ㄹ] in '사람' is a flap. In American English, flaps replace /t/ and /d/ after a stressed vowel and before an unstressed syllable.

butter	[b**ʌɾɚ**]
water	[w**ɔɾɚ**]
writer	[ray**ɾɚ**]

4. Korean Consonants

Korean consonants are also classified according to the place and the manner of articulation. As for the place of articulation, there are bilabials (ㅂ, ㅃ, ㅍ, ㅁ), alveolars (ㄷ, ㄸ, ㅌ, ㅅ, ㅆ, ㄴ, ㄹ), palatals (ㅈ, ㅉ, ㅊ), velars (ㄱ, ㄲ, ㅋ, ㅇ), and glottal (ㅎ). As for the manner of articulation, there are stops (ㅂ, ㅃ, ㅍ, ㄷ, ㄸ, ㅌ, ㄱ, ㄲ, ㅋ), fricatives (ㅅ, ㅆ), affricates (ㅈ, ㅉ, ㅊ), nasals (ㅁ, ㄴ, ㅇ), liquid (ㄹ), glides (y, w). They are shown in the following chart.

		Bilabial	Alveolar	Palatal	Velar	Glottal
stop	plain	ㅂ/p/	ㄷ/t/		ㄱ/k/	
	constricted	ㅃ/p'/	ㄸ/t'/		ㄲ/k'/	
	aspirated	ㅍ/p^h/	ㅌ/t^h/		ㅋ /k^h/	
Fricative	plain		ㅅ/s/			
	constricted		ㅆ/s'/			
	aspirated					ㅎ/h/
affricate	plain			ㅈ/ʧ/		
	constricted			ㅉ/ʧ'/		
	aspirated			ㅊ/$ʧ^h$/		
nasal		ㅁ/m/	ㄴ/n/		ㅇ/ŋ/	
liquid			ㄹ/l/			

Figure 4.1. The Consonants of Korean

Compare this with the chart of English Consonants.

Manner of Articulation	Place of Articulation													
	Bilabial		Labiodental		Interdental		Alveolar		Palatal		Velar		Glottal	
	vl	vd	vl	vd	vl	vd	vl	vd	vl	vd	vl	vd	vl	vd
Stop	p	b					t	d			k	g		
Fricative			f	v	θ	ð	s	z	ʃ	ʒ			h	
Affricate									ʧ	ʤ				
Nasal		m						n				ŋ		
Lateral								l						
Retroflex								r						
Glide		w								y		(w)		

Figure 4.2. The Consonants of English

What differences do you find between them? The most noticeable difference is that English consonants are systematically differentiated by the opposition of voicelessness and voicedness, while Korean consonants have a systematic pattern of triple opposition of plain, tense, and aspirated sounds. The difference derived from the opposition of voicelessness and voicedness is not a difference of an individual segment but a systematic difference. As Korean consonants do not distinguish between voiceless and voiced, Koreans especially find difficulty pronouncing English voiced consonants [b, d, g, v, ð, z, ʒ, ʤ].

The next is that English has more fricatives than Korean. Korean has only three fricatives [ㅅ, ㅆ, ㅎ]. Furthermore, the articulation of fricatives is more difficult than that of stops. English fricatives are challenging for Koreans to pronounce.

Korean has only one liquid /ㄹ/, while English has two liquids /l/ and /r/. The correct articulation of English /l/ and /r/ is problematic for Koreans. Besides, some other consonants which are similar but are not exactly identical to Korean consonants are also difficult for Koreans.

5. English Consonant Sounds

Unit 1 /p/ *pie*

/p/ is a voiceless bilabial stop, orally emitted. First we press our lips firmly, blocking the air. Then open our lips quickly and produce the sound with a strong puff of air.

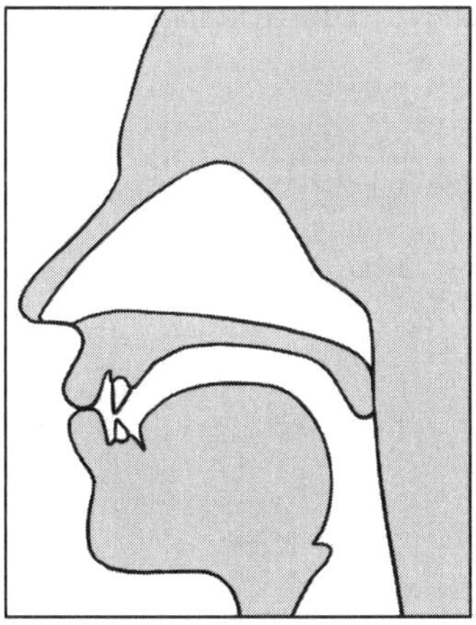

/p/

Practice 1

Listen and repeat.

/p/ /p/ /p/ /p/ /p/

Practice 2

Listen and repeat.

pie	pocket	piece
repair	appear	apart
appeal	Pinocchio	Polish
Plato	Nepal	parliament
protein	opera	

Allophones of /p/

There are various allophones of /p/ which are phonetically realized in specific environments.

- strongly aspirated $[p^{h}]$ - at stressed syllable initial (*pie*)
- weakly aspirated $[p^{|}]$ - at unstressed syllable initial (*copy*)
- unaspirated [p] - when preceded by /s/ in the same syllable (*spy*)
- unreleased $[p^{\urcorner}]$ - at word final or before another consonant, the release phase is omitted. At word final position (*cap*), it is optional but is obligatory before another consonant(*captain*).

Practice 3

Listen and repeat.

$[p^{h}]$	pie	pocket	apart
[p]	spy	speak	Spain
$[p^{\urcorner}]$	captain	aptitude	napkin

Unit 2 / b/ *book*

/b/ is a voiced bilabial stop. It is produced the same way as /p/, except /b/ is voiced. /b/ is always unaspirated and lenis.

Though both Korean [ㅂ] and [b] are lenis and unaspirated, [ㅂ] is not voiced enough to be recognized as [b]. [ㅂ] is rather recognized as [p] in the degree of voicing by native speakers of English.

We should vibrate our vocal folds when we produce /b/. If our vocal folds are to vibrate, they should be approximated when the air passes through the glottis. For /b/, native speakers approximate it — automatically without realizing they are doing it. At first Koreans automatically tend to devoice it without knowing it. We cannot move the vocal folds intentionally like our arms or legs. The vocal folds are controlled unconsciously. All Korean vowels are voiced. But no Korean is conscious of the motion of the vocal folds when we pronounce a vowel.

In order to pronounce English voiced consonants properly, three stages of practice are necessary: consciousness, separation, and application. First it is necessary to become conscious of the motion of the vocal folds. Carefully look at what you are doing, especially at your neck and larynx, when you are making other voiced sounds such as a vowel [아]. Put your fingers on your Adam's Apple and see what you are doing when you open your mouth for [아] before you say it. Slow motion is recommended. As you open your mouth, you contract your vocal folds. You make a shape for [아], constricting the vocal folds, and then expect the air to come out. When the air comes out, it will make the prepared vocal folds vibrate. If you are able to become aware of constriction, it is possible that you can constrict your vocal folds freely. This action of constriction alone is separation. If you succeeded in constriction in separation, then you have to apply constriction to consonants. As you are to pronounce a voiced consonant, you should also apply the narrowing of the vocal folds. Then the air will come out through the narrowed glottis.

For /b/, first practice /p/.

- First press your lips, blocking the air.

• Narrow your vocal folds so that the vocal folds can vibrate when the air goes through the glottis.
• Then open your lips quickly and produce the sound.

Practice 1

Listen and repeat.

/p/ /b/
/p/ /b/
/p/ /b/
/p/ /b/
/p/ /b/

Practice 2

Listen and repeat.

/b/ /b/ /b/ /b/ /b/

book	bill	bad	bourgeois
brain	bromide	black	bonus
business	butane	Beethoven	Berlin

Practice 3

Listen and repeat.

pie	buy
pack	back
peach	beach
pest	best

Practice 4

Listen and choose the word that you hear.

1. ① pat ② bat
2. ① pack ② back
3. ① pay ② bay
4. ① lab ② lap
5. ① cap ② cab

Unit 3 / t / *tie*

/t/ is a voiceless alveolar stop.

- Put the tip of the tongue against the alveolar ridge, stopping the air.
- Your tongue should not touch your teeth.
- Quickly lower your tongue, letting the air burst out.
- /t/ is similar to Korean /ㅌ/, but /t/ is further back than /ㅌ/.

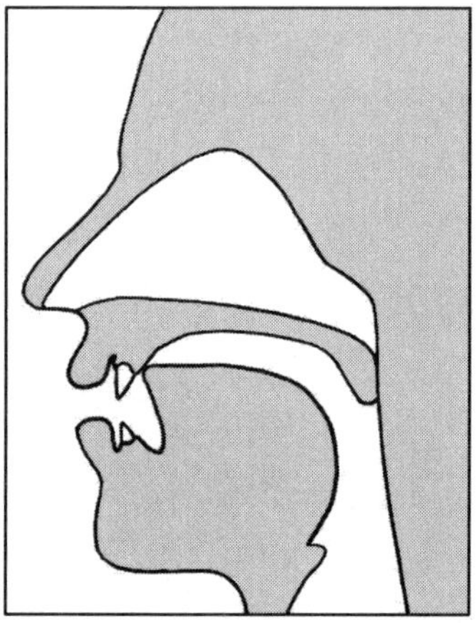

/ t /

Practice 1

Listen and repeat.

/t/ /t/ /t/ /t/ /t/

Practice 2

Listen and repeat.

[t^h]

tie	time	town	tear
attain	attempt	attend	attack

Practice 3

Listen and repeat.

[t]

stop style start story

Practice 4

[ɾ] - In American English, when it is in the environment of v___v̆, that is after a stressed vowel and before a unstressed vowel, /t/ becomes weakened to [ɾ]. [ɾ] is almost identical with Korean [ㄹ] in '사람'. [ɾ] is called a flap, because the tongue tip flaps the alveolar ridge when pronouncing it.

Listen and repeat.

atom city better water

Practice 5

[∅] - In American English, /t/ is omitted when it follows nasals.

Listen and repeat.

twenty center counter

Unit 4 /d/ *date*

/d/ is a voiced alveolar stop. It is produced the same way as /t/, except /d/ is voiced.

For /d/, first practice /t/.

- Put the tip of the tongue against the alveolar ridge, stopping the air.
- Your tongue should not touch your teeth.
- Narrow your vocal folds so that the vocal folds can vibrate when the air goes through the glottis.
- Quickly lower your tongue, making a sound.

Practice 1

Listen and repeat.

/t/ /d/
/t/ /d/
/t/ /d/
/t/ /d/
/t/ /d/

Practice 2

Listen and repeat.

/d/ /d/ /d/ /d/ /d/

Practice 3

Listen and repeat.

date	debut	down	Dracula
dance	data	drama	digital

Practice 4

Listen and repeat.

tie	die
town	down
time	dime
tear	dear

Practice 5

Listen and repeat.

bet	bed
neat	need
seat	seed
write	ride

Practice 6

Listen to these sentences. Circle the word in parentheses that you hear.

1. She likes to (ride / write) everyday.
2. I gave him my (card / cart).
3. The (tie / dye) looks great.
4. We (sent / send) all the packages by airmail.

Unit 5 / k / *cat*

/k/ is a voiceless velar stop.

- Press the back tongue against the soft palate, stopping the air.
- Then quickly lower the tongue, exploding the sound with a strong puff of air.
- The vocal folds do not vibrate.

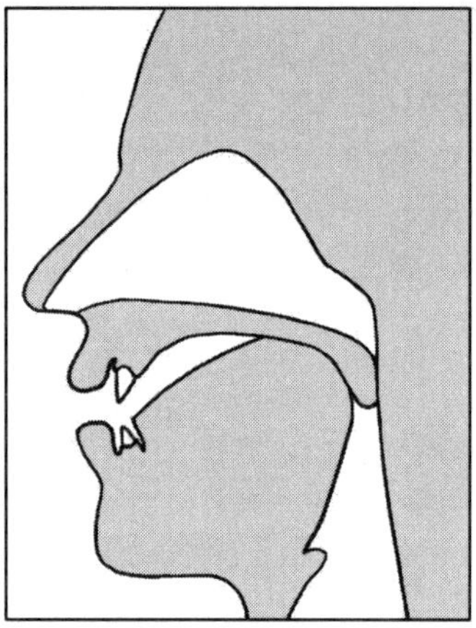

/ k /

Practice 1

Listen and repeat.

/k/ /k/ /k/ /k/ /k/

Practice 2

Listen and repeat.

camera	cake	cute	cuckoo
catholic	Bach	Cleopatra	calorie
camouflage	comma	calendar	nicotine
cocaine	chaos	cosmos	caffeine

Practice 3

Listen and repeat.

sky skate school skip

Practice 4

Listen and repeat.

bookcase factor electric doctor

Unit 6 / g / *gate*

/g/ is a voiced velar stop. It is produced the same way as /k/, except /g/ is voiced.

For /g/, first practice /k/.

- Press the back tongue against the soft palate, stopping the air.
- Narrow your vocal folds so that the vocal folds can vibrate when the air goes through the glottis.
- Then quickly lower the tongue, sounding the /g/.

Practice 1

Listen and repeat.

/k/	/g/
/k/	/g/
/k/	/g/
/k/	/g/
/k/	/g/

Practice 2

Listen and repeat.

/g/ /g/ /g/ /g/ /g/

gate	glass	game	goal	gag
yoghurt	Galilee	Niagara	jaguar	

cane	gain
cold	gold
came	game
cave	gave

Practice 3

Listen and repeat.

cap	gap
pick	pig
buck	bug
lack	lag

Practice 4

Listen to these sentences. Circle the word in parentheses that you hear.

1. That's a nice (curl / girl).
2. Did you see my (card / guard)?
3. Have you seen his new (coat / goat)?
4. There's a spider in the (back / bag).

Unit 7 / f / *food*

[f] is a voiceless labiodental fricative. Fricatives are produced by almost stopping air and forcing air out through a narrow opening. The process of releasing continues for some duration.

For /f/, touch the upper teeth with the lower lip.

- Force air out through the opening.
- Keep blowing air for some duration.
- Koreans tend to make this sound too weak with little friction or turbulence of air, confusing it with /p/. However, native speakers pronounce this very strongly.

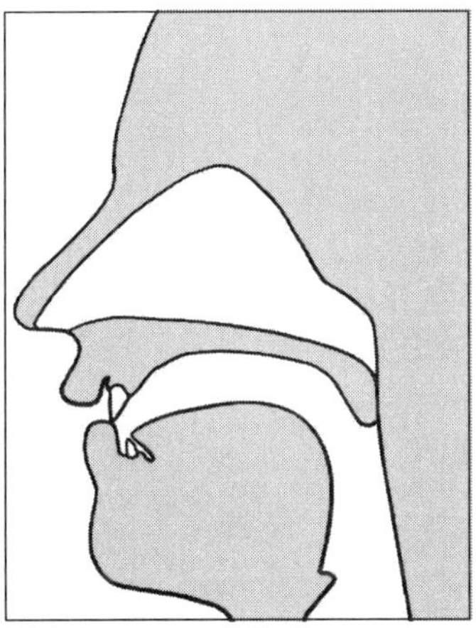

/ f /

Practice 1

Listen and repeat.

/f/	/f/	/f/	/f/	/f/
food	face	fight	fish	
caffeine	freon	sofa	buffet	
fool	pool			
fast	past			
fan	pan			
feel	peel			

chief	cheap
laugh	lap
wife	wipe

Practice 2

Listen to these sentences. Circle the word in parentheses that you hear.

1. They're worried that it's (past / fast).
2. This (cup / cuff) is dirty.
3. Please give me the (pork / fork).
4. It is (cheap / chief).

Unit 8 / v / *vase*

/v/ is a voiced labiodental fricative. It is produced the same way as /f/, except /v/ is voiced.

For /v/, first practice /f/.

- Touch the upper teeth with the lower lip.
- Narrow your vocal folds so that they can vibrate when the air goes through the glottis.
- Force air out through the opening.
- Keep blowing air for some duration.

Koreans tend to confuse /v/ with /b/. Releasing of /v/ lasts for some duration, but /b/ is released in a moment.

Practice 1

Listen and repeat.

/f/ /v/
/f/ /v/
/f/ /v/
/f/ /v/
/f/ /v/

/v/ /v/ /v/ /v/ /v/

victory	video	veil	vinyl
veranda	vitamin	Van Gogh	Wagner
Vietnam			

few	view
fan	van
safe	save
life	live

Practice 2

Listen and repeat.

base	vase
boat	vote
buy	vie
bet	vet
best	vest

Practice 3

Listen to these sentences. Circle the word in parentheses that you hear.

1. They wanted the (boat / vote).
2. Have you ever heard about the (ban / van)?
3. He's taken a (bow / vow).
4. She parked the car on the (curb / curve).

Unit 9 /θ/ *think*

/θ/ is a voiceless interdental fricative.

- Place your tongue tip between your upper and lower front teeth.
- Your upper teeth rest on your tongue.
- Force air out through the narrow opening.
- Keep blowing air for some duration.
- This sound is one of the most difficult sounds for Koreans.

Koreans tend to confuse this sound with /s/.

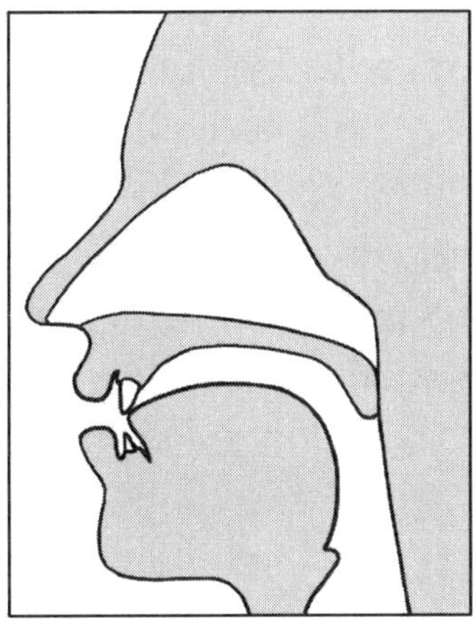

/θ/

Practice 1

Listen and repeat.

/θ/ /θ/ /θ/ /θ/ /θ/

think	theater	theme	thousand
thesis	south	theory	thank
Athens	catharsis	Catholic	marathon

Practice 2

Listen and circle the word that you hear.

1. sick	thick
2. sum	thumb
3. sink	think
4. mouse	mouth
5. pass	path

Practice 3

Listen to these sentences. Circle the word that you hear.

1. (Sink / Think) it.
2. He looks (sick / thick).
3. I like a (pass / path) through the wood.
4. This is the (sum / thumb).

Unit 10 /ð/ *they*

/ð/ is a voiced interdental fricative. It is produced the same way as /θ/, except /ð/ is voiced.

For /ð/, first practice /θ/.

- Place your tongue tip between your upper and lower front teeth.
- Your upper teeth rest on your tongue.
- Narrow your vocal folds so that they can vibrate when the air goes through the glottis.
- Force air out through the narrow opening.
- Keep blowing air for some duration.

Koreans tend to confuse /ð/ with /d/. Releasing of /ð/ lasts for some duration, but /d/ is released in a moment.

Practice 1

Listen and repeat.

/θ/	/ð/
/θ/	/ð/
/θ/	/ð/
/θ/	/ð/
/θ/	/ð/

/ð/	/ð/	/ð/	/ð/	/ð/
they	there	this	that	other
smooth	weather	together	southern	brother

Practice 2

Listen and circle the word that you hear.

1. day	they
2. dare	there
3. dose	those
4. side	scythe
5. ladder	lather

Practice 3

Listen to these sentences and circle the word that you hear.

1. It's rude to (doze / those) in a class.
2. (They / Day) will come.
3. He said, "(dough / though)".
4. She was (loading / loathing) it.

Unit 11 /s/ *sea*

/s/ is a voiceless alveolar fricative.

- Raise the tip of the tongue toward the alveolar ridge, very close to it, but without touching it.
- Putting force into your tongue, blow out air over the top of your tongue through the narrow opening, making a strong hissing sound.
- Keep blowing air for some duration.

Korean [ㅅ] is rather similar to [s]. For [ㅅ], the tongue blade is not raised, usually resting behind the lower teeth. Instead the front tongue is raised toward the alveo-palatal area.

Koreans usually confuse this sound with /θ/.

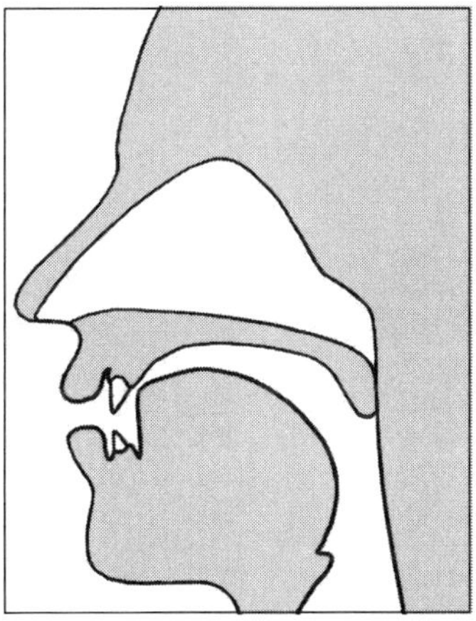

/ s /

Practice 1

Listen and repeat.

/s/ /s/ /s/ /s/ /s/

sea	city	soon	sale
suit	system	supermarket	Cinderella
Socrates	Solomon	Sweden	casino

close up	saxophone	ceramic	siren
ounce	Oedipus		

Practice 2

Listen and repeat.

thank	sank
thigh	sigh
theme	seam
myth	miss
mouth	mouse
youth	use

Unit 12 /z/ zoo

/z/ is a voiced interdental fricative. It is produced the same way as /s/, except /z/ is voiced.

For /z/, first practice /s/.

- Raise the tip of the tongue toward the alveolar ridge, being nearly close to it, but without touching it.
- Narrow your vocal folds so that they can vibrate when the air goes through the glottis.
- Giving force to your tongue, blow out air over the top of your tongue through the narrow opening.
- Keep blowing air for some duration.

Koreans tend to pronounce this sound similarly to Korean /ㅈ/. In Korean /ㅈ/, the tongue tip touches the roof of the tongue differently from English /z/.

Practice 1

Listen and repeat.

/s/	/z/
/s/	/z/
/s/	/z/
/s/	/z/
/s/	/z/

Practice 2

/z/ /z/ /z/ /z/ /z/

zoo	zebra	zero	zone	crazy
zipper	dessert	easy	xerox	
zenith	xylophone	Zurich	Zeus	

Unit 13 /ʃ/ *shampoo*

/ʃ/ is a voiceless palato-alveolar fricative.

- First practice /s/. Then move your tongue up and back a little, pushing your lips forward a little into a circle.
- Force air out over the tongue and through your teeth.

The position of the tongue for /ʃ/ is rather similar to that of Korean [ㅠㅣ], because the position of the tongue for [ㅟ] is not as high as for /ʃ/.

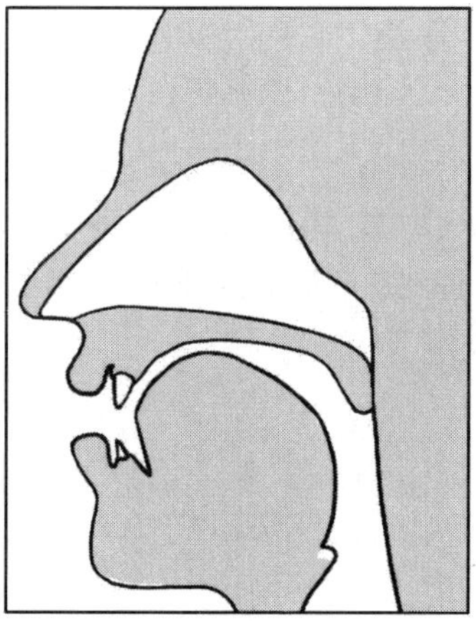

/ʃ/

Practice 1

Listen and repeat.

/ʃ/ /ʃ/ /ʃ/ /ʃ/ /ʃ/

shampoo	sugar	sure	champagne
shock	appreciate	Shakespeare	shake
Schubert	Schweitzer	Chopin	

Practice 2

Listen to these sentences and circle the word that you hear.

1. He's going to buy some new (seats / sheets).
2. Would you (sign / shine) this, please ?
3. Did he (sell / shell) all the nuts ?
4. Do you have the (lease / leash) ?
5. Those are (Sue's / shoes).

Unit 14 /ʒ/ *pleasure*

/ʒ/ is a voiced alveo-palatal fricative.

- First practice /ʃ/.
- Prepare your tongue as in Korean [쥐].
- Narrow your vocal folds so that they can vibrate when the air goes through the glottis.
- Force air out over the tongue and through your teeth.

/ʒ/ is also a difficult sound for Koreans to pronounce. The practice of articulation of /ʃ/ is prerequisite for /ʒ/.

Practice 1

Listen and repeat.

/ʃ/	/ʒ/
/ʃ/	/ʒ/
/ʃ/	/ʒ/
/ʃ/	/ʒ/
/ʃ/	/ʒ/

/ʒ/ /ʒ/ /ʒ/ /ʒ/ /ʒ/

pleasure	casual	usual	Asia
leisure	vision	luxurious	decision

Unit 15 / h / *hot*

/h/ is a voiceless glottal fricative.
/h/ is parallel to Korean /ㅎ/.

Practice 1

Listen and repeat.

/h/ /h/ /h/ /h/ /h/

hot	heart	heat	hall
humor	alcohol	hanger	Hollywood

Unit 16 /ʧ/ *choice*

/ʧ/ is a voiceless alveo-palatal affricate.
/ʧ/ is a combination of /t/ and /ʃ/.

- First put the tongue blade against the alveolar ridge, stopping the flow of air, as in /t/.
- Then lower the tongue quickly, keeping the sides of your tongue pressed against the upper back teeth and forcing air out over the tongue.
- Lips are rounded and protruding slightly.

/ʧ/ is similar to Korean /ㅊ/, but in /ㅊ/, a broad surface of the tongue touches the roof of the mouth and the lips are not protruded. The precise articulation of /ʧ/ is prerequisite for /ʤ/.

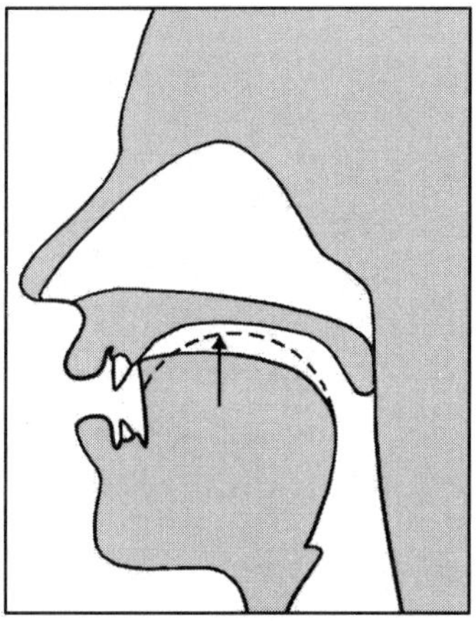

/ʧ/

Practice 1

Listen and repeat.

/ʧ/ /ʧ/ /ʧ/ /ʧ/ /ʧ/

choice	chance	cheese	cheer
chart	champion	chief	cheating

Unit 17 / ʤ / *joke*

/ʤ/ is a voiced alveo-palatal affricate.

- Put the tongue blade against the alveolar ridge, stopping the flow of air, as in /d/.
- Narrow your vocal folds so that they can vibrate when the air goes through the glottis.
- Then lower the tongue quickly, keeping the sides of your tongue pressed against the upper back teeth and forcing air out over the tongue.
- Lips are rounded and protruding slightly.

/ʤ/ is similar to Korean /ㅈ/, but different from /ㅈ/. In /ㅈ/, the broad surface of the tongue touches the roof of the mouth and the lips are not protruded.

Practice 1

Listen and repeat.

/ʧ/	/ʤ/
/ʧ/	/ʤ/
/ʧ/	/ʤ/
/ʧ/	/ʤ/
/ʧ/	/ʤ/

/ʤ/ /ʤ/ /ʤ/ /ʤ/ /ʤ/

joke	judge	Jew	jazz
juice	job	jump	journal
jam	joy	allergy	gel
hegemony	ideology	margarine	estrogen
Jehovah	Jacob	Janus	Genghis Khan

Practice 2

Listen and circle the word that you hear.

1. (Jew / zoo)
2. (jest / zest)
3. (jealous / zealous)
4. (jig / zig)

Unit 18 /l/ *light*

/l/ is a voiced alveolar lateral. There is a complete closure of the center by pressing the tongue blade against the alveolar ridge. The air escapes around the sides of the tongue, laterally emitted.

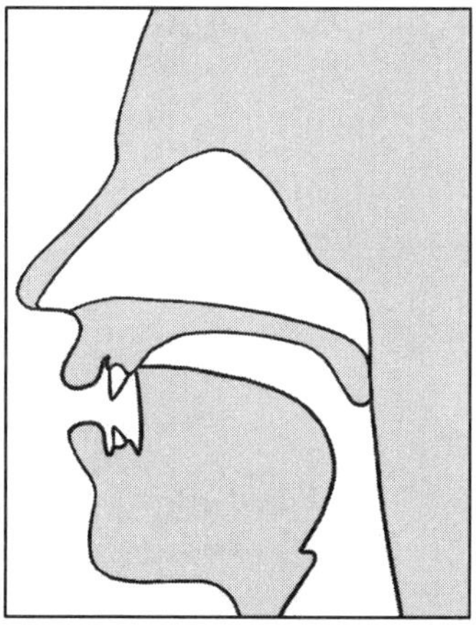

/l/

In Korean, there is only one liquid, /ㄹ/. When it is at geminate position as in '일리', /ㄹ/ is pronounced as a lateral [l]. At the rest position, such as intervocalic as in '사람' or word-initial as in '라인', /ㄹ/ is pronounced as a flap [ɾ]. The English consonant /l/ occurs as one of the allophones of /ㄹ/. Koreans tend to substitute [ɾ] for /l/ at word -initial position as in "life", "lady", etc. Try to discern what difference is between [l] and [ɾ], by pronouncing '일리' and '사람'. When you pronounce [ㄹ] of '리' in '일리', the tongue tip is nearly hard with much force and tension. In [l] of '일리', you are putting a lot of force into your tongue, while in [ɾ] of '사람', the tongue is relaxed and hits the roof of the mouth swiftly.

Practice 1

Listen and repeat.

light	left	lion	lady
loud	leader	label	leisure
license	lobbyist	level	leopard
alarm	Olympic	dilemma	

Practice 2

Listen and repeat.

[ɫ]

meal	field	help	milk
school			

Unit 19 [r] *red*

/r/ is a voiced alveolar retroflex. In a retroflex [r], the tip and blade of the tongue are raised and the tip is curled, pointing to the area behind the alveolar ridge. This is why it is also called retroflex.

- The lips may be slightly rounded or pushed out.
- Do not touch any part of the roof of the mouth when the tip of the tongue approaches the alveolar area, which is in contrast with Korean [ㄹ].

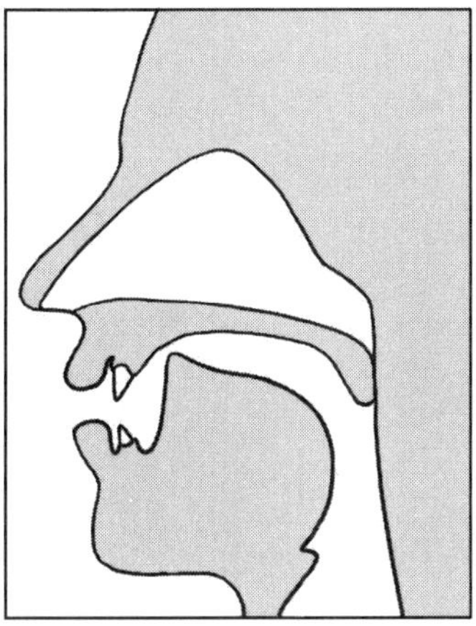

/ r /

Practice 1

Listen and repeat.

red	right	cry	free
hurry	rope	robot	racket
reader	repertory	Roosevelt	Rambo
Rockefeller	repertory	Renaissance	Rome
rabbi	Arab		

Practice 2

Listen and repeat.

race	lace
road	load
wrong	long
right	light
fry	fly

Practice 3

Listen and circle the word that you hear.

1. red / led
2. rate / late
3. rock / lock
4. crown / clown
5. erect / elect

Unit 20 / m / / n / / ŋ /

/m/, /n/, and /ŋ/ are all nasal sounds with air emitted through the nasal cavity. Differences between them are caused by the point at which the air is obstructed in oral cavity.

/m/ is a voiced bilabial nasal. The air is stopped bilabially by closing your lips.

• Let the air flow out through your nose.

/n/ is a voiced alveolar nasal. The air is stopped alveolarly by pressing the tip of your tongue against the alveolar ridge.

• Let the air flow out through your nose.

/ŋ / is a voiced velar nasal. The air is stopped at the velum by raising the back of your tongue and pressing it against the roof of your mouth.

• Let the air flow out through your nose.

Korean has three parallel nasal consonants: [ㅁ], [ㄴ], [ㅇ].

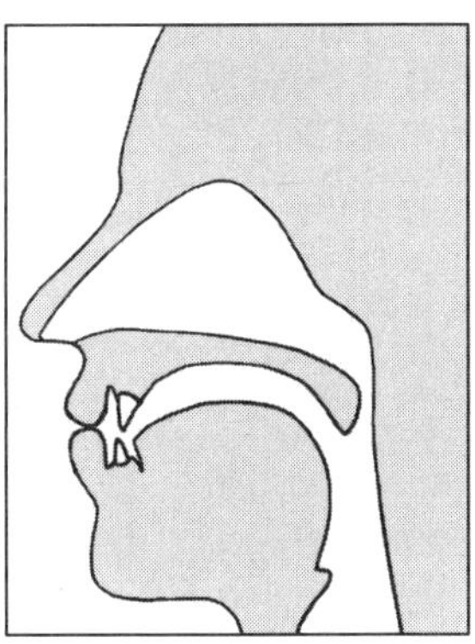

/m/

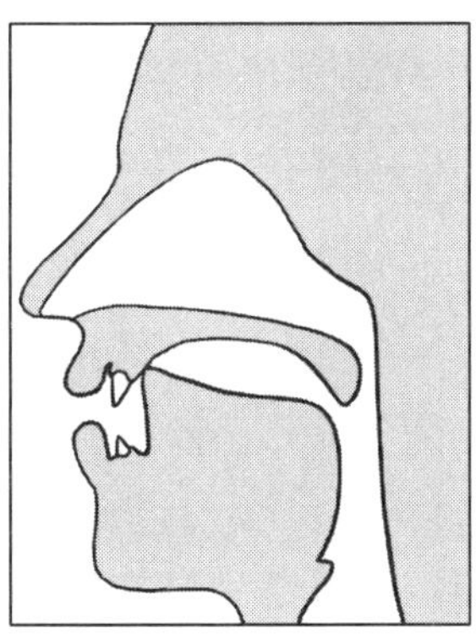

/n/

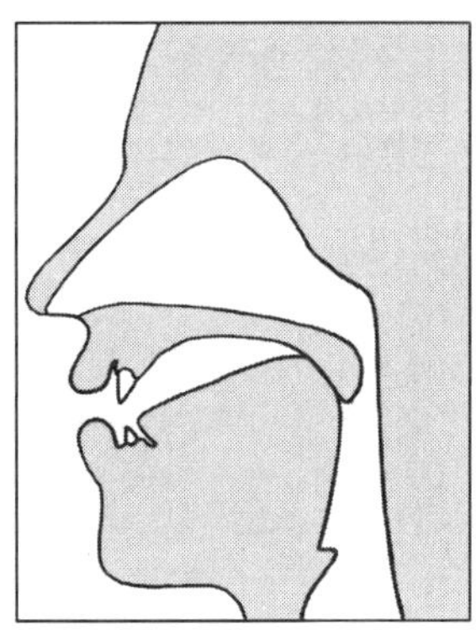

/ŋ/

Practice 1

Listen and repeat.

/m/

Mom	music	manner	matter
move	Mozart		

/n/

nice	note	never	niece
Nobel			

/ŋ/

long	thing	bank	anchor
lung			

Unit 21 / y / / w /

/y/ is a voiced palatal glide.
/w/ is a voiced bilabial glide.

[y] is made like [i] with a slight closure in the palatal region, but shortly it glides into the following articulation position. It is classified as a palatal glide.

[w] is made like [u] by raising the back of the tongue toward the velum while rounding the lips at the same time. It is classified as a bilabial/velar glide.

Korean has [y] as in '야' [ya], '여', [yʌ], '유' [yu], etc and [w] as in '와' [wa], '위' [wi], '워' [wʌ], etc. They are relatively easy.

In Korean, there are no sequences such as [yi] and [wu]. They are difficult for Koreans. Koreans tend to omit [y] in *yeast* or *yield*. In this case, the position of the tongue for [y] is further higher and more advanced than that of the following vowel [i]. Koreans also tend to delete [w] in *wool* or *wood*. Likewise the position of the tongue for [w] is further higher and more retracted than the following vowel [u].

Practice 1

Listen and repeat.

[y]

yes	you	yeast	yield	yet

[w]

win	war	wood	won't	wool

6. Description of English Vowels

6.1 Phonetic Symbols for English Vowels

Before we discuss English vowels, let us consider their phonetic symbols. There have been different systems of phonetic alphabets to represent English vowel sounds though phonetic alphabets used in dictionaries[2)] may be the most familiar to Koreans. The phonetic alphabet adopted in this book is listed in the chart below. Where American English (AE) and British English (BE) are different for some vowel sounds, symbols for vowel sounds of British English are also given in the next column. Dictionary symbols are also listed at the far right of the horizontal row of the vowel sound if they are different.

symbol	BE	Words	dictionary
/iy/		leave	/i:/
/ɪ/		live	/i/
/ey/		paper	/ei/
/ɛ/		bell	/e/
/æ/		hat	

2) Phonetic symbols in Daniel Jones' (1956) *An English Pronouncing Dictionary* are usually adopted in dictionaries.

symbol	BE	Words	dictionary
/uw/		food	/u:/
/ʊ/		look	/u/
/ow/		no	/ou/
/ɔ/		ball	
/ɑ/	/ɒ/	not	
/ə/		banana	
/ər (ɚ)/	/ə:/	brother	
/ɜr (ɝ)/	/ɜ/	bird	/ə:r/
/ʌ/		cup	
/ay/		fine	/ai/
/ɔy/		boy	/ɔi/
/aw/		house	/au/

6.2 Articulation of English Vowels

Vowels are the most audible sounds in speech. This property of the vowels is reflected in their Korean name, '모음', whose literal meaning is 'mother sound', while the name of consonants is '자음', 'child sound'. Vowels function as a head of a syllable. Most consonants depend on the vowel for their audibility. For example, in the word *cup*, neither [k] nor [p] has much sound of its own. If we separate the sound waves of consonants from the vowel acoustically and listen to each, they are not recognizable as [p] or [k] sounds, but they are just popping sounds. Consonants are mainly perceived by the way they affect the beginning and end of the vowel sound.

Vowels are produced with a relatively open vocal tract, so they do not have a place of articulation or manner of articulation as with consonants. Also, all English vowels are voiced. Therefore, vowels should be described in terms of criteria different than those used for consonants. The sound wave for vowels is made by vocal fold vibration, which is the sound source. A specific vowel is determined by its unique shape of the vocal tract above the glottis. That is, the shape of the vocal tract determines which vowel is produced - [i]. [u], or [a], for example. Speakers change the shape of the vocal tract with the tongue and the lips to produce different vowels by doing as follows:

1. raising or lowering the body of the tongue
2. advancing or retracting the body of the tongue
3. rounding or not rounding the lips
4. making these movements with tense or lax gestures

English vowels are described according to these four aspects of the articulation of the vowel. The tongue positions for vowels are represented in the following chart for English vowels as well as Korean vowels.

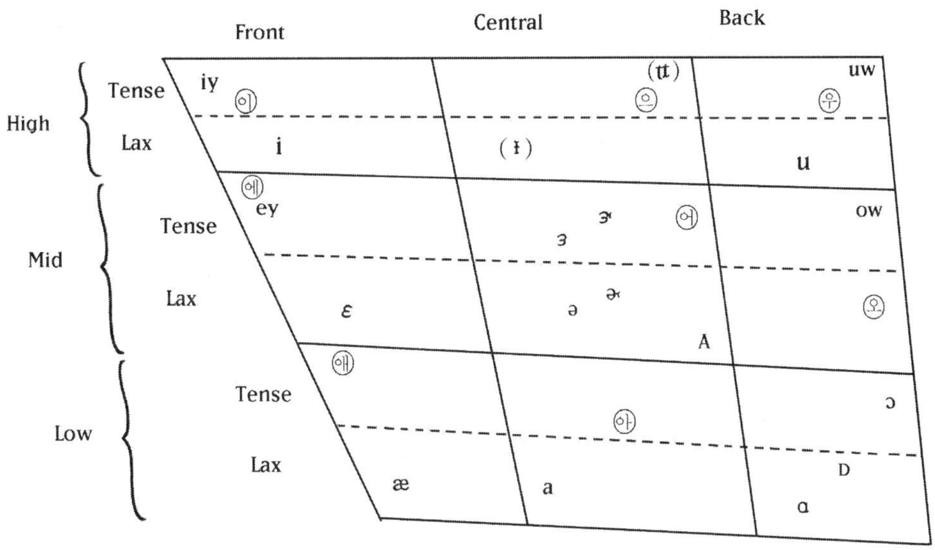

Figure 6.1 The Chart of English Vowels

6.2.1 Tongue Height

We change the shape of the vocal tract inside the mouth by raising or lowering the body of the tongue. If we say vowels [이] and [애], we will find that we open our mouth wider as we change from [이] to [애]. These varying degrees of openness correspond to different degrees of tongue height. In English, [iy] is high, [ɛ] mid, and [æ] low.

High vowels are made with the mouth less open and the tongue body raised. The high vowels of English are [iy, ɪ, uw, ʊ]. Mid vowels are produced with an intermediate tongue height. In English, mid vowels are [ey, ɛ, ɜ, ə, ʌ, ow]. Low vowels are made with the mouth open and the tongue lowered. [æ, a, ɑ, ɔ] are low vowels in English.

6.2.2 Tongue Advancement

We can also change the shape of the oral cavity by pushing forward or pulling back our tongue. For example, in [iy], the body of the tongue is advanced and it is just under the hard palate. In contrast, in [uw], the tongue is retracted toward the velum. [iy, ɪ, ey, ɛ, æ] are front vowels where the body of the tongue is pushed forward, while [uw, ʊ, ow, ɔ, ɑ] are back vowels in that they are made with the body of the tongue retracted. Central vowels, [ə, ʌ, ɜ], require neither fronting nor retraction of the tongue.

6.2.3 Tenseness

In English vowels, muscular tension of the vocal organs like the tongue and the lips is important in determining vowel quality. Tense vowels are differentiated from lax vowels by degrees of muscular tension. Tense vowels require considerable muscular tension of the vocal organs, especially the tongue. On the other hand, lax vowels are made without force of the vocal organs and the tongue is relaxed while they are being articulated. The contrasts between [iy](*seat*) vs. [ɪ](*sit*), [ey](*late*) vs. [ɛ](*let*), [uw](*fool*) vs. [ʊ](*full*) are all due to the difference of such tension. [iy, ey, uw, ow] are tense vowels and [ɪ, ɛ, ʊ] are lax vowels.

Tense vowels are made with more extreme position of the tongue than their counterpart lax vowels because of the tension of the tongue. For example, the tongue position for the vowel [iy] is higher and more advanced than for the vowel [ɪ]. In lax vowels, the tongue is lowered and retracted due to its looseness. Tense vowels also tend to be lengthened, being all diphthongs such as [iy, ey, uw, ow].

All Korean vowels are slightly tensed. Korean vowels are not distinguished on the basis of tenseness or laxness. That means that tenseness of the tongue is not a distinguishing feature for determining vowel quality in the Korean language. If we pronounce the Korean vowel [이] either in a strongly tensed way or in a very relaxed way in '이름' (*name*), it is recognized as the same vowel, meaning the same word. Both sounds are perceived as the same vowel and they do not cause a difference in meaning. Koreans do not have any concept about tenseness as far as vowels are concerned. And as tensing of muscular organs is made unconsciously, Koreans do not know how to differentiate tense vowels from lax vowels. They do not know how to make vowels tense and how to make vowels lax if they are not trained phonetically.

Are there any ways Koreans can experience tensing of muscular organs and can recognize what muscular tension is? If so, they can learn how to make tense vowels or lax vowels. Fortunately, there are ways Koreans can experience muscular tension, though it does not happen during the articulation of vowels. Korean consonants show a triple opposition pattern as in /ㅂ, ㅃ, ㅍ/, /ㄷ, ㄸ, ㅌ/, /ㄱ, ㄲ, ㅋ/, /ㅈ, ㅉ,ㅊ/. Korean consonants are distinguished with regard to plain, tense, aspirated consonants. For tense consonants, the concerned vocal organs are tensed. Plain consonants are made just plainly without aspiration or tension. Pronounce pairs of plain consonants and tense consonants, /ㅂ, ㅃ/, /ㄷ, ㄸ/, /ㄱ, ㄲ/, and /ㅈ, ㅉ/, trying to find out consciously what you are doing when you pronounce a plain consonant and its tense counterpart consonant. When you pronounce tense consonants, you give a great deal of force to our concerned vocal organs. When we pronounce /ㅃ/, we give a lot of force into the lips and close them firmly in contrast with /ㅂ/. When we pronounce /ㄸ/, we put a lot of force into our tongue and press it to the roof of the mouth tightly in contrast with /ㄷ/.

If we give more force into the tongue which is held in the position for the Korean vowel /이/, just as if we are going to pronounce /ㄸ/, then we are making a tense vowel /iy/. Reversely for the lax vowel /ɪ/, we should remove our force from the tongue which is in the position for the Korean vowel /이/. So when we pronounce the lax vowel /ɪ/, the state of the tongue blade is like that of the tongue in rest position.

6.2.4 Lip Rounding

Vowel quality is also affected by the lip shape. The lips may be rounded or spread. In [uw] as in *fool*, the lips are rounded. In [iy] as in *east*, they are unrounded. Vowels with rounded lips are named rounded vowels, while vowels with spread lips are called unrounded vowels. English has four rounded vowels: [uw, ʊ, ow, ɔ]. The other vowels in English are unrounded.

6.3 Diphthongs

[ay] as in *ice*, [aw] as in *town*, and [ɔy] as in *boy* are diphthongs. They consist of a vowel and a glide, forming one syllable. Vowels are the head of the syllable. Glides cannot be the head of the syllable, because glides do not last long enough. Thus, *ice* is one syllable word with [a] syllabic and [y] non-syllabic.

6.4 Exercise

1. Provide the phonetic symbol which is represented by the following descriptors.

   a. high front lax vowel
   b. mid back tense vowel
   c. low back lax vowel
   d. mid front tense vowel
   e. low front lax vowel

2. Provide the appropriate three-part articulatory descriptions for the following vowel sounds.

   a. [iy]
   b. [uw]
   c. [ɛ]
   d. [ɔ]
   e. [ə]
   f. [ʊ]

3. Transcribe the following words.

   a. linguistics
   b. prefix
   c. profile
   d. sure
   e. vowel
   f. log
   g. adjective
   h. preface
   i. women
   j. unless
   k. half
   l. consonant
   m. access
   n. boot
   o. adverb
   p. phonetics

7. English Vowel Sounds

Unit 1 / iy / *east*

- /iy/ is a tense front high vowel.
- Raise the front part of your tongue high in your mouth close to the roof.
- The muscles of your tongue should be tense. Press the sides of your tongue against the upper molar teeth, spreading your lips firmly.
- As you say /i/, move the front part of your tongue forward and up for /y/.
- The tongue position for /i/ is higher and more advanced than for Korean /이/ because /iy/ is produced more tensely than /이/. Open your mouth just like Korean /이/ and give a lot of force to the tongue and the lips.

Practice

Listen and repeat.

/iy/ /iy/ /iy/ /iy/ /iy/

east	see	mean	leaf
easy	heat	neon	key
elite	meeting	Eden	Aesop
amoeba	caffeine		

Unit 2 /ɪ/ *it*

- /ɪ/ is a lax front high vowel.
- The front part of your tongue is high in your mouth, a little lower and less advanced than for the sound /iy/.
- The muscles of vocal organs—the tongue and the lips—should be relaxed.
- The tongue position for /ɪ/ is lower and more retracted than for Korean [이] because /ɪ/ is more relaxed than [이]. Open your mouth just like Korean /이/. Holding the tongue position, remove all force from your tongue and lips so that the state of your tongue becomes a resting position as when we breathe. Say it shortly.

Practice 1

Listen and repeat.

/ iy /	/ ɪ /
/ iy /	/ ɪ /
/ iy /	/ ɪ /
/ iy /	/ ɪ /
/ iy /	/ ɪ /

/ ɪ / / ɪ / / ɪ / / ɪ / / ɪ /

it hill sit kid isn't ticket

heat	hit
seek	sick
leave	live
feat	fit
reach	rich
read	rid
meal	mill
least	list

Practice 2

Listen and circle the word that you hear.

1. (sheep / ship)
2. (leap / lip)
3. (deed / did)
4. (beat / bit)
5. (feel / fill)

Unit 3 /ey/ *say*

- /ey/ is a tense front mid vowel.
- Raise the front tongue in the middle of your mouth, a little lower than for /iy/ and /ɪ/.
- Lower your jaw and your lips more than for /ɪ/.
- The muscles of your tongue should be tense. Press the sides of your tongue against the molar teeth.
- Add the glide /y/.
- The tongue position for /e/ is higher and more advanced than for Korean [에] because /e/ is produced more tensely than [에]. Open your mouth just like Korean /에/ and give more force to your tongue and lips. Add sound /y/.

Practice

Listen and repeat.

/ey/ /ey/ /ey/ /ey/ /ey/

say	late	great	make
paper	stapler	crayon	veil
rein	weigh	oasis	mosaic
label	serenade	radio	

Unit 4 /ɛ/ egg

- /ɛ/ is a lax front mid vowel.
- The front part of your tongue is in the middle, a little lower than for /ey/.
- Lower your jaw and your lips more than for /ɪ/.
- The muscles of vocal organs—the tongue and the lips—should be relaxed.
- The tongue position for /ɛ/ is lower and more retracted than for Korean [에] because /ɛ/ is more relaxed than [에]. Open your mouth just like Korean /에/. Holding your tongue position, remove all force from your tongue so that the state of your tongue becomes a resting position as when we breathe. Say it shortly.

Practice 1

Listen and repeat.

/ey/	/ɛ/
/ey/	/ɛ/
/ey/	/ɛ/
/ey/	/ɛ/
/ey/	/ɛ/

/ɛ/ /ɛ/ /ɛ/ /ɛ/ /ɛ/

egg	let	wet	sell	get	says
any	friend	preface	meant	medal	cleansing
level	leopard				

Practice 2

Listen to these sentences and circle the word that you hear.

1. His (pen / pain) is awful.
2. I want to (sell / sail) the boat.
3. The coffee tastes (bitter / better).
4. They're talking about their (debt / date).
5. Can I have some (pepper / paper) ?

Unit 5 / æ / hat

- /æ/ is a front low vowel.
- Lower your jaw more than for /ɛ/.
- /æ/ is lower than Korean /애/. Open your mouth a little more than for /애/.
- /æ/ and /ɛ/ are difficult for Koreans to distinguish.
- Some words pronounced as [æ] in American English (AE) are pronounced as [ɑ] in British English (BE).

Practice 1

Listen and repeat.

/ɛ/	/æ/
/ɛ/	/æ/
/ɛ/	/æ/
/ɛ/	/æ/
/ɛ/	/æ/
/ɛ/	/æ/

/æ/	/æ/	/æ/	/æ/	/æ/
hat	cat	gas	black	
pamphlet	catalog	category	man	
ballet	marathon	salad	sad	
calorie	aspirin			

Practice 2

Listen and repeat.

met	mat
lend	land
very	vary
merry	marry
beg	bag
bed	bad

Practice 3

Listen and repeat, paying attention to difference in pronunciation between AE and BE.

	AE	BE
ask	[æsk]	[ɑsk]
task	[tæsk]	[tɑsk]
pass	[pæs]	[pɑs]
class	[klæs]	[klɑs]
dance	[dæns]	[dɑns]
laugh	[læf]	[lɑf]
half	[hæf]	[hɑf]
bath	[bæθ]	[bɑθ]
aunt	[ænt]	[ɑnt]
basket	[bæskɪt]	[bɑskɪt]
answer	[ænsər]	[ɑnsə]

Practice 4

Listen to these sentences and circle the word that you hear.

1. She bought a (pen / pan).
2. He (left / laughed) when she didn't come.
3. That man in the picture is (dead / dad).
4. They are (said / sad) to be leaving.
5. Did you hear about the (bet / bat) ?

Unit 6 /uw/ *who*

- /uw/ is a tense back high round vowel.
- Raise the back of your tongue toward the soft palate.
- Round your lips.
- The muscles of your tongue should be tense.
- As you say /u/, move the back part of your tongue backward and up for /w/.
- The tongue position for /u/ is higher and more retracted than for Korean /우/ because /uw/ is produced more tensely than /우/.
- Open your mouth just like Korean /우/ and put more force into your tongue and lip.

Practice

Listen and repeat.

/uw/ /uw/ /uw/ /uw/ /uw/

who	two	suit	move
soup	fool	do	pool

Unit 7 /ʊ/ cook

- /ʊ/ is a lax back high round vowel.
- Raise the back of your tongue toward the soft palate, but lower than for the sound /uw/.
- Round your lips slightly.
- The muscles of vocal organs – the tongue and the lips – should be relaxed.
- The tongue position for /ʊ/ is lower and more central than for Korean [우] because /ʊ/ is more relaxed than [우]. Open your mouth just like Korean /우/. Holding the tongue position, remove all force from your tongue and lips so that the state of your tongue becomes a resting position as when we breathe. Say it shortly.

Practice 1

Listen and repeat.

/uw/ /ʊ/
/uw/ /ʊ/
/uw/ /ʊ/
/uw/ /ʊ/
/uw/ /ʊ/

/ʊ/ /ʊ/ /ʊ/ /ʊ/ /ʊ/

cook	wool	wood	good
foot	took	put	cook
push	woman		

Practice 2

Listen and circle the word that you hear.

1. (fool / full)
2. (pool / pull)
3. (suit / soot)
4. (who'd / hood)
5. (stewed / stood)

Unit 8 /ow/ *hope*

- /ow/ is a tense back mid round vowel.
- Lower your jaw and open your lips more than for /ʊ/.
- The muscles of your tongue should be tense.
- Add the glide /w/.
- The tongue position for /o/ is higher and more retracted than for Korean [오] because /o/ is produced more tensely than [오]. Open your mouth just like Korean /오/ and give more force to your tongue and lip. Add sound /w/.

Practice

Listen and repeat.

/ow/ /ow/ /ow/ /ow/ /ow/

hope	no	boat	low
goal	coke	trophy	profile
omega			

Unit 9 / ɔ / *all*

- /ɔ/ is a back low vowel.
- Open your mouth more than for /o/ (a little more than for Korean /오/).
- Round the lips slightly.

Practice 1

Listen and repeat.

/ɔ/	/ɔ/	/ɔ/	/ɔ/	/ɔ/
long	saw	all	law	boss
cost	ball	hall	talk	orange

Practice 2

Listen and repeat.

bought	boat
caught	coat
walk	woke
called	cold
raw	row
clause	close
cost	coast
lawn	loan

Practice 3

Listen to these sentences. Circle the word in parentheses that you hear.

1. They fell in the (hall / hole).
2. She dropped the (ball / bowl).
3. Were they (called / cold)?
4. We (walk / woke) early in the morning.

Unit 10 /ɑ/ father

- /ɑ/ is a back low unround vowel.
- Open your mouth the most of any English vowel. Open your mouth as you do to the doctor, saying [아 ~].
- /ɑ/ is lower and more retracted than Korean /아/.

Practice 1

Listen and repeat.

/ɑ/ /ɑ/ /ɑ/ /ɑ/ /ɑ/

father	hot	top	doctor
drama	job	comedy	cosmos
model	opera	lobby	copy
monitor	boycott	Oscar	

Unit 11 /ɒ/ hot

- /ɒ/ is back low round vowel.
- /ɒ/ is lower than /ɔ/. First practice /ɑ/ and then round your lips.
- In British English, most words spelled 'o' are pronounced with this sound. /ɑ/ is generally substituted for this vowel in General American.

Practice

Listen and repeat.

/ɒ/ /ɒ/ /ɒ/ /ɒ/ /ɒ/

(British English)

hot not stop bomb doctor body

Unit 12 /ʌ/ *cup*

- /ʌ/ is a central mid lax vowel.
- Lower your jaw a little more than for Korean [어]. Open your mouth enough that your thumb can get in.
- The muscles of the tongue are relaxed. Be careful not to put force into your tongue as in Korean /어/. Say it shortly.

Practice 1

Listen and repeat.

/ʌ/ /ʌ/ /ʌ/ /ʌ/ /ʌ/

cup	touch	money
cut	couple	luck

Practice 2

Listen and circle the word that you hear.

1. (dawn / done)
2. (boss / bus)
3. (long / lung)
4. (gone / gun)
5. (dog / dug)

Unit 13 /ə/ *ago*

- /ə/ is a central mid lax vowel.
- First practice /ʌ/, then make it very short. This is /ə/.
- /ə/ is a very short sound. It is always unstressed.
- The position of the tongue is neither raised nor lowered, neither advanced nor retracted, being in the rest position without any tension. Say it shortly.
- /ə/ is more front and relaxed than Korean /어/.
- /ə/ is called schwa. In English, almost all vowels in unstressed syllables are weakened or obscured to /ə/. So /ə/ is also called the reduced vowel or obscure vowel. As there are more unstressed than stressed syllables, /ə/ is among the most frequently heard vowel sounds.

Practice

Listen and repeat.

/ə/ /ə/ /ə/ /ə/ /ə/

ago	above	opera	famous
camera	second	salad	terrific
fragile	lemon	today	police
potato	purchase	lettuce	
barometer	telepathy	academy	

Unit 14 /ər (ɚ)/ *teacher*

- /ər/ is pronounced as /ɚ/ in American English as in *doctor, actor, etc.*
- /ɚ/ is a retroflex vowel with r-coloring added to /ə/.
- Open your mouth a little with the tongue in the rest position and the tip of the tongue curled a little for /ɚ/.
- The muscles of the tongue are relaxed.
- In British English, /ə/ is pronounced without r-coloring.

Practice

Listen and repeat.

/ɚ/ /ɚ/ /ɚ/ /ɚ/ /ɚ/

teacher	tutor	labor
color	after	sister

Unit 15 /ɜɾ (ɝ)/ *work*

- /ɜr/ is a stressed vowel of /ər/ as in *work, bird, etc.*
- /ɜr/ is pronounced as /ɝ/ in American English.
- In British English, /ɜ/ is pronounced without r-coloring.

Practice

Listen and repeat.

/ɝ/ /ɝ/ /ɝ/ /ɝ/ /ɝ/

work	person	girl	turn
perfect	learn	courage	worry
burn	world		

Unit 16 /ay/ /aw/ /ɔy/

- /ay/, /aw/, /ɔy/ are diphthongs.
- /a/ is a central low lax unround vowel.
- The tongue is more front for /a/ than for Korean /아/.

Practice

Listen and repeat.

/ay/	/ay/	/ay/	/ay/	/ay/
fine	ice	fly	sigh	wife
/aw/	/aw/	/aw/	/aw/	/aw/
now	out	doubt	town	brown
/ɔy/	/ɔy/	/ɔy/	/ɔy/	/ɔy/
voice	joy	choice	coin	noise

8. Word Stress

8.1 Syllable

So far we have considered consonants and vowels. Let us move to a larger unit, a syllable. A syllable is a constituent unit of a word, though "글자" is used informally instead of a syllable in Korea. For example, the word '축제' consists of two "글자" or two syllables, '자전거' three syllables. A syllable is a constituent of a word that contains one vowel sound.[3)] It may also contain one or more consonant sounds. In general, the number of vowel sounds corresponds to the number of syllables in a word.

Practice

Write down the number of the syllables of the following words.

1. cup
2. support
3. wait
4. vowel
5. homework
6. radio
7. rose
8. sister
9. potato
10. consonant
11. boat
12. condolence

---

3) A consonant sometimes forms a syllable by itself after another consonant, without a vowel between them, as in *bottle*, *middle*, *button*. The sounds /l/ and /n/ are the most common syllabic consonants.

8.2 Word Stress

In English, in every word with two or more syllables, every syllable is not equally weighed phonetically, but one syllable is stressed. The stressed syllable is **louder, higher in tone, and longer.** Each word has one stressed syllable.[4] Other syllables are less stressed or weak (unstressed) syllables. The unstressed syllable is weaker, lower in tone, and shorter. This is different from many languages where syllable strength is nearly equal for all syllables.

Trager and Smith (1951) distinguish four kinds of relative stresses.

primary stress : / ́/
secondary stress : / ̂/
tertiary stress : / ̀/
weak stress : / ̆/

With this notation, the word *preparation* is transcribed as prèpăration, the phrase *white house* ('house of white color') as whîte hóuse. This textbook adopts primary stress (/ ́/), secondary stress (/ ̂/), and tertiary stress (/ ̀/). There are also different kinds of stresses such as phrase stress or nuclear stress and sentence stress.

8.3 Two-Syllable Words

Practice 1

Listen and repeat.

a. Stress on first syllable
1. **vi**-sit
2. **pa**-per
3. **En**-glish
4. **e**-ven
5. **ad**-verb

4) All one-syllable content words such as *come*, *want*, *stop*, etc have a word stress in phrases.

b. Stress on second syllable

1. to-**day**
2. po-**lite**
3. in-**stead**
4. be-**tween**
5. com-**pare**

Practice 2

Underline each stressed vowel of the words below.

1. easy	4. correct	7. become
2. o'clock	5. measure	8. hundred
3. mistake	6. exit	9. after

Practice 3

One partner says 3 two-syllable words. The other partner writes them down, with a mark on the stressed vowel. Try this in turn.

1.
2.
3.

8.4 Three-Syllable Words

Practice 1

Listen and repeat.

a. Stress on first syllable

1. **ho**spital	4. **ci**tizen	7. **ac**cident
2. **em**phasis	5. **si**milar	8. **mi**neral
3. **for**tunate	6. **a**djective	9. **con**sonant

b. Stress on second syllable

1. e**di**tion
2. a**ban**don
3. ad**ven**ture
4. to**mo**rrow
5. **ima**gine
6. in**su**rance
7. dis**tin**guish
8. pa**ja**mas
9. de**po**sit

c. Stress on third syllable

1. under**stand**
2. disa**ppoint**
3. after**noon**
4. engi**neer**
5. intro**duce**
6. repre**sent**

Practice 2

Underline each stressed vowel of the words below.

1. factory
2. mechanic
3. comparable
4. suspicious
5. eraser
6. policy
7. paternal
8. delicious
9. register

Practice 3

One partner says 3 three-syllable words. The other partner writes them down, with a mark on the stressed vowel. Try this in turn.

1.
2.
3.

8.5 Four-Syllable Words

Practice 1

Listen and repeat.

a. Stress on first syllable

1. **in**teresting
2. **li**terature
3. **tem**porary
4. **ce**remony
5. **a**micable
6. **se**cretary

b. Stress on second syllable

1. de**mo**cracy
2. im**me**diate
3. ge**o**graphy
4. cer**ti**ficate
5. co**me**dian
6. con**ve**nient

c. Stress on third syllable

1. inde**pen**dent
2. manu**fac**ture
3. uni**ver**sal
4. decla**ra**tion
5. senti**men**tal
6. prepo**si**tion

Practice 2

Underline each stressed vowel of the words below.

1. January
2. original
3. parenthesis
4. ordinary
5. particular
6. cafeteria
7. necessary
8. political
9. encyclopedia

9. Compound Word Stress

A compound word is made up of two or more words. A compound word is written together as one word ('passport') or as two separate words ('post office'). In compounds, the primary stress is usually placed on the first word component.

9.1 Compound Noun /ˊ +ˋ/

A. Noun + Noun /ˊ +ˋ/

1. spacebar
2. seatbelt
3. sports car
4. lady doctor (부인과 의사) cf. lâdy dóctor (여의사)

B. Adjective + Noun /ˊ +ˋ/

1. greenhouse (온실) cf. green house (/ ˆ + ˊ /) (푸른 집)
2. social worker (사회복지사)
   cf. social worker (/ ˆ + ˊ /) (사교적인 직원)
3. English teacher (영어 선생님)
   cf. English teacher (/ ˆ + ˊ /) (영국인 선생님)

C. Gerund + Noun /´ +`/

1. dancing floor (무도장)
   cf. dancing girl (/ ˆ + ´ /) (춤을 추고 있는 소녀)
2. moving van (이사용 밴)
   cf. moving van (/ ˆ + ´ /)
3. sleeping car (침대차)
   cf. sleeping baby (/ ˆ + ´ /)

9.2 Compound Adjective /´ +`/ 5)

1. breath taking
2. home made
3. duty free

Practice

Underline the primary stress in the following compound words.

1. blueprint	4. software
2. traffic light	5. credit card
3. world wide	6. air conditioner

5) The stress pattern is /` + ´ / for *adjective* + *past participle* like *funny-shaped*, *near-sighted*, etc.

10. Stress in Words with Affixes

There are two kinds of affixes with relation to the stress pattern of base word. One kind of affix preserves the stress pattern of the base when it is added to a base. The other kind of affix shifts the stress pattern of the base, prescribing the primary stress to a particular syllable position.

10.1 Preserving Affixes

When they are added to a base, the stress pattern of the base word remains the same.

A. Suffixes

1. - ment	agree	agreement
2. - ness	happy	happiness
3. - able	reason	reasonable

B. Prefixes

Most prefixes are preserving affixes.

1. un-	fortunate	unfortunate
2. dis-	agree	disagreement
3. auto-	biography	autobiography

10.2 Shifting Affixes

When a shifting affix attaches to the word, the stress pattern of the base word changes.

1. -tion	contribute	contribution
2. -ic	democrat	democratic
3. -ity	possible	possibility
4. -ian	Paris	Parisian

Practice

Write your own base word and its affixed word in the blanks. Mark the stress notation on the stressed syllable.

	base word	affixed word
1. -ly		
2. -ical		
3. -ity		
4. -sion		

11. Reduced Vowels in Unstressed Syllables

11.1 Vowels in Unstressed Syllables

There exists more discrimination between stressed and unstressed syllables in English than in most other languages. In English, unstressed vowels do not have a full form of a vowel sound; /a/, /e/, /i/, /o/, /u/. Instead they are reduced to schwa, /ə/ or /ɪ/. In most cases, schwa appears in unstressed vowels. Schwa is articulated with the least effort. The tongue is in the rest position. The vowel sound is very short.

Practice

Listen and repeat.

1. compare
2. suppose
3. polite
4. agenda
5. seven
6. husband
7. famous
8. sentence
9. medicine
10. disappear
11. fortunate
12. mineral

Many languages of the world do not have vowel reduction. Neither does Korean. Koreans may think that vowel reduction is too casual.

Sometimes Koreans make the mistake of pronouncing unstressed vowels as full vowels in an anxiety to make themselves understood. The opposite is true. Reduced vowels are more natural and correct.

11.2 Unstressed Vowels in Conversion

There are words which may be used either as nouns or verbs without a change in their spelling. That is, verbs are converted into nouns without any suffix. The verb and the noun have the same spelling, but their stresses are different. The noun has its primary stress on the first syllable, while the verb has on the last in two syllable words. Stress is assigned to a different syllable, depending on whether it is a noun or a verb. This stress also affects qualities of vowels in the word. It determines whether the vowel is pronounced as a full or a reduced vowel.

Practice 1

First write the meaning of each word in Korean. Listen and repeat.

	Verb	meaning	Noun	meaning
1. contest	contest [kəntɛ́st]		contest [kɑ́ntɛst]	
2. contract	contract [kəntræ̍kt]		contract [kɑ́ntrət]	
3. desert	desert [dɪzɝ́rt]		desert [dɛ́zɚt]	
4. increase	increase [ɪnkríys]		increase [ɪ́nkriys]	

Practice 2

Provide each word with its meaning and phonetic transcription.

	verb	meaning	noun	meaning
1. present				
2. progress				

3. survey				
4. suspect				
5. insult				

Practice 3

One partner says either (a) or (b). The other partner says the rest sentence.

1. a. We negotiated a CONtract.
   b. Our muscles conTRACT when we exercise.
2. a. They made a lot of PROgress.
   b. Let's proGRESS to the next goal.
3. a. Please handle the OBject carefully.
   b. I obJECT to the proposal.
4. a. They cannot deSERT him.
   b. They reached the DEsert.
5. a. He'll reCORD his message.
   b. This is off the REcord.
6. a. We need a PERmit to go there.
   b. Please perMIT me to go there.

Practice 4

Mark the primary stress on all words.

1. No one suspected that suspects would be killed.
2. They protested an increase of overtime work.
3. You are a convert when you convert from one religion to another.
4. Though the conflict is over, they still continue to conflict with each other.
5. He would object if I gave her a present.

11.3 Words ending with -ate

English words that end with *-ate* may be used as adjectives, nouns, or verbs. In case of an adjective or a noun, *-ate* is unstressed. Thus *-ate* is pronounced as [ɪt] or [ət]. When it is used as a verb, *-ate* gets a secondary stress, being pronounced as [eyt].

Practice 1

Provide each word with its meaning and phonetic alphabets.

	Noun/ Adjective	meaning	verb	meaning
1. alternate				
2. animate				
3. elaborate				
4. moderate				
5. deliberate				
6. intimate				
7. separate				
8. graduate				
9. estimate				

Practice 2

Listen and repeat the above words.

Practice 3

One partner says either of two sentences. Then the other partner says the other sentence.

1. We graduate next month.
   They are graduate students.

2. They alternate in doing dishes.
   You are advised to use an alternate route.
3. They estimate it will cost $ 500.
   I'd like to know an estimate of the cost.
4. They separated after dinner.
   We need a separate office.
5. The opposition was deliberate.
   They want to have time to deliberate.
6. She prepared a very elaborate dinner.
   She wanted to elaborate upon the idea.

Practice 4

Transcribe each word phonetically.

Canada		Canadian	
politics		political	
history		historical	
sincere		sincerity	
prepare		preparation	
atom		atomic	
telegraphy		telegraphic	

12. Sentence Stress

Just like there is stress differentiation among syllables in English words, there is also differentiation among words in sentences. English words have parts which are strong (stressed syllables) and parts which are weak (unstressed syllables). In the same way, English sentences have parts which are strong (stressed words) and parts which are weak (unstressed words).

In sentences, strong parts and weak parts are determined by word class. Contents words occupy strong parts and function words weak parts. Speakers of English unconsciously manipulate their utterances and highlight contents words and obscure function words. Content words are usually nouns, verbs, adjectives, and adverbs. They express the main content of the sentence. Sentence stresses are placed on the content words by giving more strength to them. The content words are made easier to hear, helping listeners to get the sense of the sentence. On the other hand, function words are articles, pronouns, prepositions, auxiliary verbs, and conjunctions. These words are generally not stressed. They have structural meaning, which can be predicted in the context.

The verbs *be* and *have* are unstressed even when they are the principal verb in the sentence:

1. (a) Máry is my bést fríend.
   (b) Kárl has a lóvely cár.

On the other hand, they are stressed when they come at the end of a sentence and when they are used in tag question. Negative forms like *don't, isn't, doesn't, hasn't* are stressed.

2. (a) I thóught you were smárter than what you áre.
   (b) You háven't máde anóther cáll, háve you?

Practice 1

Circle the content words in the following sentences.

1. We drew up the contract.
2. The woman is talking on the phone.
3. Do you have a driver's license ?
4. They felt a connection.

Sentence stresses are determined simply by applying this principle.

Practice 2

Mark the stress on the words in the below sentences.

1. He will succeed in a business.
2. In an hour it will be ready to submit to you.
3. I don't think he is to resign.
4. He was sacrificed by the tyranny of big presses, wasn't he?

If contrastive meaning is intended, that word receives sentence stress even if it is a function word. For example, if not *she* but *he* is meant in *He will succeed in a business, he* is stressed: *Hé will succéed in a búsiness.*

Usually in telegrams, only content words are used because of the cost per word. For example,

3. Coming 12th
   Pick Up Airport

The telegram means: I am coming on the 12th.
Pick me up at the airport.

This telegram style is similar to the type of sentence stress.

Practice 3

1. Write a telegram with your own message, using only content words.

   ____

2. Exchange your telegram with your partner. Guess and fill out missing function words in your partner's telegram.

   ____

   ____

Practice 4

Listen and repeat the following sentences. Then mark the stress on the words.

1. Today is the eighth of August.
2. The schedule is arranged for the students.
3. Get ready for the test.
4. The class started on Tuesday.

13. English Rhythm

The Korean language is a syllable-timed language. Every syllable is considered as having about the same length and force. The syllable is a determining unit for rhythm in traditional Korean poems. For example, for the typical rhythm, a line is composed of words in order: for example, 3-syllable word, 4-syllable word, 3-syllable word, and 4-syllable word. A word of three syllables comes first and then a word of four syllables follows it (3 4). As this again repeats (3 4), the rhythm is created in the line. The rhythm is created by the repetition of a specific number of syllables.

In contrast, English is a stressed-timed language. English rhythm has respect to stress, not syllable. Stressed syllables keep a regular interval. From one stressed syllable to the following stressed syllable is of about the same length and force. There is nearly equal time between the sentence stresses. Stressed syllables tend to recur at about the same interval, creating rhythm. The rhythm in English is based on the regular recurrence of stressed syllables.

Consider the following three sentences.

1 a. Boys / need / money.
b. Boys / will need / some money.
c. Boys / will be needing / some money.

The sentence (1a) consists of 4 syllables, while (1c) 8 syllables. Sentence (1c) is twice as long as (1a) in terms of syllables. For Koreans, (1c) needs almost twice the time that (1a) needs because Koreans measure sentences based on syllables. However, all three sentences have the same number of sentence stresses. Every sentence (1a), (1b), and (1c) carries three sentence stresses. The sentence (1a), (1b), and (1c) are of the same length from a viewpoint of stress. Native speakers of English pronounce each of these three sentences in about the same length of time because they measure sentences based on stress.

How could it be made possible to pronounce two sentences in the same length of time when one sentence is long and other sentence is short ? The answer is that native speakers unconsciously crush together the unstressed syllables in order to keep regular intervals. Koreans usually find it very hard and uncomfortable to crush together unstressed syllables.

When speakers say stressed-timed sentences, they do two different jobs simultaneously:

- Give emphasis to stressed syllables.
- Weaken unstressed words and syllables, obscuring the vowels in most of them.

While speakers are doing both jobs, they are aiming to make stressed syllables recur rather regularly. For example, consider the following telegram and its intended sentences again.

2 a. Coming 12th
Pick Up Airport

b. I am coming on the 12th.
Pick me up at the airport.

(2b) is much longer than (2a), but try to say both sentences in the same length of time.

Practice 1

Listen and repeat the following sentences. There is nearly equal time between the sentence stresses.

1. Coming 12th
   I am coming on the 12th.

2. Pick Up Airport
   Pick me up at the airport.

Practice 2

Listen and repeat the following sentences. There is nearly equal time between the sentence stresses.

1. Boys / need / money.
2. Boys / will need / some money.
3. Boys / will be needing / some money.

14. Reduced Words

Function words of one syllable have both a strong form and a weak form in pronunciation. The strong form occurs when they are pronounced by themselves and receive stress. The weak form arises when they are used in sentences and do not receive sentence stress. When they are unstressed, their vowels are reduced, resulting in a form different from a strong form. Function words are usually used together with other words. Thus, weak forms are commonly used forms in speech. They are what you hear and speak in communication. The weak forms are very important and natural. Function words of one syllable are among the most commonly used words — especially *the, of, and, to, a, in, that, it, is, I* . These ten words make up 25 percent of all English. ESL students should train themselves to hear and understand weak forms when they are used in the natural conversational speech.

Practice 1

Listen and repeat.

Function Words	Strong Form	Weak Form	Examples
a	[ey]	[ə]	Read a book.
and	[ænd]	[ənd], ['nd], ['n]	back and forth

Function Words	Strong Form	Weak Form	Examples
are	[ɑr]	[ər]	What are you doing?
have	[hæv]	[həv],[əv], [ə] [v]	Where have you been?
has	[hæz]	[həz] [əz] [ə] [z]	Where has he been?
had	[hæd]	[həd] [əd] [d]	What had he studied?
of	[ɑv]	[əv] [ə]	in front of
for	[fɔr]	[fər]	Thanks for calling me.
or	[ɔr]	[ər]	two or three
to	[tuw]	[tə]	go to work
at	[æt]	[ət]	at home
as	[æz]	[əz]	as far as I know
that	[ðæt]	[ðət]	now that I know
can	[kæn]	[kən]	I can do it.
because	[bɪkɔz]	[bəkəz]	because we want
was	[wɑz]	[wəz]	I was absent.
will	[wɪl]	[wəl]	I will do that.
from	[frɔm]	[frəm]	far from here

Practice 2

Draw a line through the unstressed function words.

1. What are our chances?
2. Ask for a raise.
3. Are we having classes on Friday?
4. Today is my pay day.
5. I'll come at three or four.
6. Does this bus go downtown?
7. How do you say that in English?

Practice 3

Listen to the sentences and write the word you hear in the blank.

1. Where did __________ go ?
2. Please give __________ the tickets.
3. She brought __________ food.
4. I'd like this more __________ that.
5. We need one __________ two.
6. When __________ he come back ?
7. What __________ you do last week ?
8. I ______________ known him for years.
9. The waiter must __________ mixed up the orders.
10. This work is new ____ me.
11. Is it ________ sale ?
12. Turn ___________ the next corner.
13. Do in Rome _______ the Romans do.
14. I missed the beginning __________ the movie.

can is reduced to [kən], but *can't* is pronounced as [kænt]. When the final /t/ of *can't* is unreleased, a person would understand it as negative or positive depending on whether he heard /æ/ or /ə/. Reversely if you fail to obscure the *a* of *can*, you may be understood to say "can't", which is the opposite of what you intended.

Practice 4

Listen to these sentences. Circle the word in parentheses that you hear.

1. I (can't / can) stand on my head.
2. He (can't / can) play the guitar.
3. (Can't / Can) you help me?
4. He (can't / can) speak French, but his sister (can't / can).
5. I (can't / can) meet you tomorrow.

15. Linking

In speech, there is no space between words as there is writing. Words are not pronounced as separate units. Rather, they are joined and blended together within a thought group. They flow continuously on outward breath. The sound of the last word is connected to the beginning sound of the next word without stopping after each word. The blending between the two words of *put it* is as close as that between the two syllables of *putting*. This joining and blending of words is also called linking.

Practice 1

Listen and repeat.

1. today
   to try
   to town
2. at any price
   of the peace
   was a beauty
3. the rest of us
   proud of it
   fan of hers
4. all of a sudden
   out of order
   date of birth

Practice 2

The following transcription show phrases in speech with blending well done. Write them out in ordinary spelling.

1. [ɪnəbʌs]
2. [ɪzəfrɛnd]
3. [ayədɵɔt]
4. [fayvɚsɪks]
5. [ðɔzðətkeym]
6. [ʃɪəztowldmɪ]

16. Contraction

Contractions are frequently used in speech. In contraction, two words are shortened and combined into one form as in *don't*. Contracting proceeds as follows. First, a vowel is reduced to schwa. Then sounds may be more weakened into the omissions of consonants or vowels or both. Then the remaining sounds lose its position as an independent word and must be linked to the words on one or both sides.

The contractions are both natural and correct in spoken English. They may be used in informal written English.

Practice 1

Listen and repeat.

1. He's gone.
2. She's worked for an hour.
3. John'll go with us.
4. Why're you asking ?
5. When're you calling ?
6. How've you been ?
7. I could've gone with her.
8. I must've seen her.
9. I should've called him.
10. He might've seen her.

Some contractions are found in spoken language, but not in written form. Contractions are usually related to the collapse of weak forms of function words. This kind of contracted form is heard in natural conversational fast speech.

Practice 2

Listen and repeat.

1. I like'er very much.
2. I like'im very much.
3. I like'em very much.
4. Does'e know'er ?
5. Where'd'e go ?

Some contracted spoken forms, which are never written, undergo sound changes due to the influence of neighboring sounds. They are also heard in natural spoken English. Some examples are below. The spellings are used here just to represent their pronunciations for convenience.

Practice 3

Listen and repeat.

1. I wanna have a break.
2. We're gonna have a break soon.
3. He hasta finish his report.
4. I hafta work on Sunday.
5. Gimme a break, uh?

17. American English and British English

English is nowadays used as a formal language in the world. It is a first language in England, the USA, Canada, Australia, New Zealand. There are also South African English and Philippine English. There exist substantial differences among American English, British English, South African English, etc. There are also dialectal variations in English used in one country.

17.1 Received Pronunciation and General American

Although "Standard English" is not formulated in England and America, *Received Pronunciation* in British English and *General American* in American English are supposed to correspond to the concept of standard English. Received Pronunciation (RP) is mostly adopted among educated people in England. RP refers to the pronunciation in everyday conversation by people with higher education, living in London. Since RP is mostly used by people of high and middle class, it is also associated with social class. About 10 % of the population uses RP.

General American is used by people from Ohio through the middle western states to the Pacific coast. About two thirds of the USA population use *General American*. Besides GA, there are an Eastern dialect in New England states like Massachusetts, Connecticut, Vermont, etc., and a Southern dialect in southern states like Texas, Louisiana, Alabama, Florida state, etc. GA is rather a regional accent, not a social class accent. Differences in pronunciation between American English (AE) and British English (BE) will be considered based on GA and RP.

17.2 Vowel Differences

Differences between AE and BE exist more greatly in vowels than in consonants.

First, postvocalic *r*'s in / ɪr, ɛr, ʊr, ɔr, ɑr, ər, ɜr / are dropped in RP. Instead the preceding vowel tend to be pronounced as a centering diphthong without r-coloring ([ɪə, ɛə, ʊə, ɔə]) or be lengthened ([ɑ:, ɜ:]). In GA r-coloring is usually added to the preceding diphthongs or vowels ([ɪɚ, ɛɚ, ʊɚ, ɔɚ, ɑr, ɚ, ɝ]).

Practice 1

Listen and repeat.

	AE	BE
beer	[bɪɚ]	[bɪə]
air	[ɛɚ]	[ɛə]
sure	[ʃʊɚ]	[ʃʊə]
door	[dɔɚ]	[dɔə]
start	[stɑrt]	[stɑ:t]
brother	[brɑðɚ]	[brɑðə]
bird	[bɝd]	[bɜ:d]

Second, some [æ]s in GA, as in *ask*, are pronounced as [ɑ]s in RP.

Practice 2

Listen and repeat.

	AE	BE
ask	[æsk]	[ɑsk]
half	[hæf]	[hɑf]
class	[klæs]	[klɑs]
chance	[ʧæns]	[ʧɑns]
dance	[dæns]	[dɑns]
demand	[dɪmænd]	[dɪmɑnd]
pass	[pæs]	[pɑs]

Third, some [ɑ]s in GA, as in *not*, are pronounced as [ɒ]s in RP.

Practice 3

Listen and repeat.

	AE	BE
not	[nɑt]	[nɒt]
top	[tɑp]	[tɒp]
stop	[stɑp]	[stɒp]
box	[bɑks]	[bɒks]
doll	[dɑl]	[dɒl]

Fourth, some [ɔ]s in GA, as in *cross*, are pronounced as [ɒ]s in RP.

Practice 4

Listen and repeat.

	AE	BE
cross	[krɔs]	[krɒs]
talk	[tɔk]	[tɒk]
long	[lɔŋ]	[lɒŋ]
taught	[tɔt]	[tɒt]
ought	[ɔt]	[ɒt]

As mentioned above, [ɚ] in GA, as in *brother,* is pronounced as [ə] in RP, and [ɝ] in GA, as in *bird,* is pronounced as [ɜ]s in RP.

Practice 5

Listen and repeat.

	AE	BE
brother	[brʌðɚ]	[brʌðə]
doctor	[dɑktɚ]	[dɒktə]
actor	[æktɚ]	[æktə]
sugar	[ʃʊgɚ]	[ʃʊgə]
better	[bɛtɚ]	[bɛtə]

	AE	BE
bird	[bɝd]	[bɜd]
girl	[gɝl][6]	[gɜl]
first	[fɝst]	[fɜst]
earth	[ɝθ]	[ɜθ]
nurse	[nɝs]	[nɜs]

6) Words like *girl*, *world*, *twirl*, *hurl* are mostly pronounced as 2 syllables in GA.

17.3 Consonant Differences

There are not many differences in consonants. Postvocalic *r* is not pronounced in BE as mentioned in the above. In AE, /t/ is optionally pronounced as [ɾ] when it is in the environment of v́__v̌. That is, when it is located after a stressed vowel and before an unstressed vowel, /t/ becomes weakened to [ɾ] (attest *[əɾɛst], a test *[əɾɛst]).

AE	
/t/ -> [ɾ]	city [sɪɾɪ] letter [lɛɾər] atom [æɾəm] hit 'im [hɪɾɪm] right or wrong [rayɾɚrɔŋ]

In AE, /t/ is omitted when it is in the environment of v́n__v̌. That is, when it follows /n/ coming after a stressed vowel and before an unstressed vowel, the release of /t/ is made nasally. It is made possible since /n/ and /t/ have the same point of articulation.

AE	
/t/ -> [n]	twenty [twɛnɪ] center [sɛnɚ] winter [wɪnɚ] Atlanta [ətlænə] painted [peynɪd]

In the case of consonant clusters, /y/ as part of the diphthongal vowel is often omitted in AE when it follows alveolar consonants such as /t, d, n/.

	AE	BE
due	[duw]	[dyuw]
new	[nuw]	[nyuw]
tune	[tuwn]	[tyuwn]

Answers

5. English Consonant Sounds

Unit 2 /b/ Practice 4

1. ① 2. ② 3. ① 4. ② 5. ②

Unit 4 /d/ Practice 6

1. ride 2. card 3. tie 4. sent

Unit 6 /g/ Practice 4

1. curl 2. card 3. coat 4. bag

Unit 7 /f/ Practice 2

1. fast 2. cup 3. fork 4. cheap

Unit 8 /v/ Practice 3

1. boat 2. van 3. bow 4. curb

Unit 9 /θ/ Practice 3

1. Think 2. sick 3. path 4. sum

Unit 10 /ð/ Practice 3

1. doze 2. They 3. though 4. loading

Unit 13 /ʃ/ Practice 2

1. sheets 2. shine 3. sell 4. lease
5. shoes

Unit 17 /ʤ/ Practice 2

1. zoo 2. jest 3. jealous 4. zig

Unit 19 /r/ Practice 3

1. led 2. rate 3. lock 4. clown
5. erect

7. English Vowel Sounds

Unit 2 /ɪ/ Practice 2

1. sheep 2. lip 3. did 4. beat
5. fill

Unit 4 /ɛ/ Practice 2

1. pain 2. sell 3. better 4. date
5. pepper

Unit 5 /æ/ Practice 4

1. pan 2. laughed 3. dead 4. sad
5. bet

Unit 7 /ʊ/ Practice 2

1. full 2. pool 3. suit
4. hood 5. stood

Unit 9 /ɔ/ Practice 3

1. hole 2. ball 3. cold 4. woke

Unit 12 /ʌ/ Practice 2

1. done 2. bus 3. long 4. gone
5. dug

14. Reduced Words

Practice 3

1. he
2. her
3. him
4. than
5. or
6. did
7. did
8. have
9. have
10. to
11. for
12. at
13. as
14. of

Practice 4

1. can
2. can't
3. can
4. can't, can
5. can't